You can eat well, even healthy, on a low-cost budget! Your family can do it, because we do it!—from the Introduction

"Practical and easy to read. I recommend [Rhonda Barfield's] methods to anyone wanting to eat better for less."
—Mary Hunt, editor of *Cheapskate Monthly* newsletter and author of *The Best of Cheapskate Monthly* and *The Cheapskate Monthly Makeover*

"If feeding your family for only $50 a week seems like an impossible dream, wake up and meet Rhonda Barfield."
—Sarah Casey Newman, Food Columnist, *St. Louis Post-Dispatch*

Rhonda Barfield and her six member family have done it themselves—developed, tested, and used methods for cutting their weekly food budget, keeping good nutrition a priority! She shares it all with you in EAT HEALTHY FOR $50 A WEEK.

You'll learn:

- how to identify the excuses you're using *not* to save money and change them into simple reasons *to do it*
- how to shop smart at supermarkets and grocery stores, then save even more with coupons, refunding, and bulk buying
- how to get the most out of food cooperatives
- how to save time and cook a whole month's worth of meals—in one day
- Plus dozens of delicious and healthy low-cost recipes, complete with nutritional analyses, and much, much more, to help you EAT HEALTHY FOR $50 A WEEK.

A Selection of the Better Homes & Garden Book Club

D0019071

Eat Healthy for $50 a Week

Feed Your Family Nutritious, Delicious Meals for Less

BY
RHONDA BARFIELD

KENSINGTON BOOKS

Food Guide Pyramid: A Guide to Daily Food Choices. Courtesy of the U.S. Department of Agriculture, Center for Nutrition Policy and Promotion.

Peak Season for Fruits and Vegetables reprinted with permission from *The Frugal Times* (September 92).

KENSINGTON BOOKS are published by

Kensington Publishing Corp.
850 Third Avenue
New York, NY 10022

Kensington and the K logo Reg. U.S. Pat. & TM Off.

First Kensington Printing: March, 1996
10 9 8 7 6 5 4 3

ISBN: 1-57566-018-0

Printed in the United States of America

CONTENTS

Find out why the Barfields cut their spending on groceries from almost $100 to $50 a week, and how that savings helped them to realize a dream in their lives. Read about the family's conversion to healthier eating, and the reasons behind the change.

Learn Rhonda's methods for saving money at the store • Check out her shopping list • Read the menu plans that follow.

Save Money on What You Buy (Meats; Dairy Foods; Produce; Breads, Grains, Pasta, Cereals) • Bulk Buy From Warehouse Stores • Try THE PANTRY PRINCIPLE™ • Use Coupons • Do Refunding.

Belong to a Cooperative • Barter (National Commercial Exchange; SHARE) • Get Organized (Meal Plan; Do Once-a-Month Cooking; Mega-Cook®; Use Leftovers; Try 24-Hour-in-Advance Meal Planning; Do 15-Minute Cooking) • Make or Cook Your Own (Meats and Other Proteins; Dairy Foods; Breads, Grains, Pasta, Cereals; Other Foods) • Garden

(Extension Services; Gardening Books and Publications; Garden Clubs and Associations) • Preserve Your Food (Freezing; Canning) • Glean • Benefit from Government Programs • Eat Sensibly.

ACKNOWLEDGMENTS

My sincere thanks go to Nancy Castleman, Marc Eisenson, Marcy Ross, Jackie Iglehart, Candace Magruder, and Anneliese Thomas for their thorough proofreading and constructive criticism of many passages in this text. Toni Lopopolo, my agent, deserves credit for selling my manuscript. JoAnn Knapp, Sally Davis, and Jan Kent researched many recipes and shared them freely. Beth Lieberman, my editor, was both encouraging and stimulating. Carol Schlitt, Extension Educator of Nutrition and Wellness at the University of Illinois Cooperative Extension Service, did me the *great* favor of nutritionally analyzing all my recipes at no cost; I am most grateful. Many others— most of them named in the text—contributed by offering expert advice and information. I appreciate all the loving input.

Thank you, Mother, and mother-in-law Marilyn, for some wonderful recipes and cooking tips through the years. I am always inspired by your good examples of thriftiness.

I'm especially grateful to my long-suffering husband and dearest friend, Michael, for encouragement, computer support, and long Monopoly games with our children. Thank you, too, Eric, Christian, Lisa, and Mary, for putting up with Mom on the days when I tried to write, and you kept busy elsewhere!

Eat Healthy for $50 a Week is dedicated to those who want to eat good, nutritious foods, yet save back extra cash—as we did—in order to realize dreams in their lives.

INTRODUCTION

Welcome to *Eat Healthy for $50 a Week*

Does this title sound familiar to you? If so, perhaps you've heard of my original book, *Eat Well for $50 a Week*. You may even know the story behind it: how my family of six cut our grocery bill in half, from almost $100 to $50 a week, in order to help bail us out of both a financial crisis and a bad neighborhood.

Throughout our 22 years of marriage, my husband Michael and I have never made much money. Michael is an artist, and my training and background is in music. Both of us broke The Unofficial Law of the Arts: Never marry an artist (or a musician) unless *you've* got a great-paying job! Still, though we've always been relatively poor, our lives have been good.

Several years ago, however, we began a financial tailspin. It started when both of us quit our jobs in order to interview for better positions in other parts of the country. We had several good leads on employment and were sure we could move right into solid careers. But it didn't work out that way at all. As we traveled to West Virginia, North Carolina, and Florida, we charged food, car repairs, and interview expenses on credit cards. (We know now how foolish this was, but didn't think it was then.)

We were unemployed for nearly a year. Eventually I was hired to teach at a piano school and Michael freelanced in art. Then came children, four in six years. Michael went to work for a publishing company, but wasn't paid well. When my part-time, insurance company employer gave me an ultimatum—work full-time or be laid off—I chose to leave and stay home with the children. By that time, money was *really* tight.

In spite of serious financial problems, our lives were peaceful, at least for a while. Then our apartment complex began to deteriorate, and rapidly. In one year's time the area changed, as newcomers moved in and most others moved out. There were rumors of a crack house down the street, and burglaries everywhere. One night as we slept, someone nearly broke in through our bedroom window.

We wanted to leave but simply didn't have the money. Bringing in more cash was not a possibility at the time. And how could we ever afford the higher rent needed for a nice house in a better part of town? We analyzed our budget over and over again, trying to think of some way to squeeze out an extra hundred dollars or more a month.

At last we decided to trim our food budget. It wasn't much, but by paring our spending from nearly $100 down to $50 a week, we were soon able to afford a lovely three-bedroom home with nearly four times the space of our cramped apartment. For $200 more a month (in additional rent and utilities), our family now lives comfortably and safely.

I think you can see how voluntarily limiting our food spending has made such a difference in our lives. By cutting our grocery bill in half, we now have something much more important to us than steaks and microwave dinners.

Still, saving money isn't everything. And now my story continues.

You see, three years ago, when Michael and I self-published *Eat Well for $50 a Week*, I was convinced that we really ate *well*. In reading through four weeks of "real-life menus" I recorded in my book, many agreed. A registered dietician looked over my meals and commented, "Although these menus may not exactly meet all the recommended dietary guidelines, when balancing budget, food preferences of children, and dietary considerations, they are adequate and realistic."

Others strongly disagreed. One nutritional expert went so far as to say, "I find it hard to believe that any registered dietician would approve of the way your family eats."

Ouch! That hurt! And the worst part of it was this: if I could not demonstrate that *we* ate well on our budget, maybe *nobody* could eat well on a thrifty budget. Perhaps every family should make high spending on food a priority, and trim back in less important areas. If so, then I certainly had no business counseling others to cut their grocery budgets while undermining their good nutrition!

You can imagine how confused I felt. I had always believed my knowledge of proper nutrition was, at least, better than average. Now I realized that I had much to learn. I began to read, whenever I could fit in a chapter or even a paragraph or two. I'm afraid I uncovered just enough information to confuse me even further.

I read, for example, that some authors advocated strict vegetarianism as a means of eating healthy. Some vegetarians recommended no dairy products, others did. Some experts insisted you must eat your foods in a certain order, such as fruit only in the mornings, fresh vegetables for lunch, etc. Some were adamant about serving only organic foods and whole grains. Some suggested no more than 30 percent fat in one's diet, while others demanded no more than 20 percent, or even 10 percent. Some recommended no sugar, or limited sugar, or honey, or sugar substitutes, or none of the above . . . and the list went on.

Even worse, none of these books seemed very "kid friendly." Many of the recipes were incredibly complicated, overly exotic or simply awful-sounding. I could have *served* them to my family, but was sure the dishes would never be *eaten.* (Would your children gobble down "artichoke hearts on a bed of vegetables?!") The end result of my initial research discouraged me from trying to change *anything* in our diet. This was just too hard!

And then, gradually, I began to recognize some common themes of good nutrition in much of what I was reading. These themes were confirmed when a registered dietician at Barnes Hospital, here in St. Louis, did an overall analysis of my menus and recommended that my family improve our diet as follows:

1. Use fewer foods high in hidden fat.
2. Increase fruits and vegetables, including a good vitamin C source daily. (Recommended servings are three to five vegetables and two to four fruits a day.)
3. Increase low-fat dairy products as children need three servings daily.
4. Try to increase fiber content of menus with the inclusion of more whole grain breads, cereals, rice, and increased amounts of fruits and vegetables as previously suggested.

5. Possibly use more dried beans and other low-cost protein sources to enhance protein content of menus.

At last, I had some kind of tangible, reasonable goals to work toward. And now, the important question: could I incorporate a healthier way of shopping and cooking into our lifestyle, one which my family would support, and still do it for $50 a week? I resolved to try. Over three years' time, we gradually made some changes in our diet. Here's how my family converted to a new way of eating.

1. We cut our consumption of red meat—and in turn, much saturated fat—by two-thirds. Instead, we eat more chicken, fish, and nearly vegetarian meals. I prepare more nutritious, low-fat desserts, and eliminate most of the oil called for in many baked goods. I replace regular margarine with low-fat margarine, or whenever possible, with canola and olive oil, and try to avoid excess fat altogether. We eat more baked and broiled—and very few fried—foods. We also cut out most high-fat snack foods, such as potato chips and cheese curls.
2. We try to eat at least "5 a day for better health," as the American Cancer Society recommends, referring to fruits and vegetables. We now buy almost exclusively frozen and fresh fruits and vegetables, mostly from a local produce stand, where we know they're as fresh as possible. I serve most fruits and vegetables raw, or steam or Crock-Pot® veggies, in order to better preserve nutrition.
3. We keep nonfat powdered milk on hand and mix extra portions into baked goods and other foods (such as salmon croquettes) when possible, to increase the children's number of dairy servings. I take a calcium supplement. Many of our desserts are not only low-fat, but also dairy-based.
4. I use oats in nearly everything I bake, and/or oat flour and whole wheat flour. I buy and serve brown rice, potatoes, whole grain whole wheat bread and bran cereal as much as possible. Homemade bread from my bread machine always contains whole grain flour.
5. We have increased our weekly servings of beans, and plan to eat more in the future.

I might add that we've also cut our sugar content considerably, though this has been difficult. (We're all sugar addicts.) We've decided not to use many substitutes, just eat less sweeteners overall.

So far, we've been successful in significantly improving our diet and keeping our weekly grocery bills at $50 to $55. Have the Barfields attained perfection? No, not at all. But we continue to try to cut back on fat, and increase servings of fruits, vegetables, low-fat dairy products, whole grains, and beans. I believe we're following a healthy middle ground, as far as nutritional theory goes.

In summary, then: although the fine points of nutrition may seem mind-boggling, some basic principles of good eating can be understood and applied. *You can eat well, even eat healthy, on a low-cost budget!* Your family can do it, because we do it!

How? The next chapter (and Appendix One) outlines four shopping lists and three weeks of our new-and-improved menu plans, in order to give you a starting point for personalizing your own plans. Please keep in mind that my lists were never intended to be the Great Master Plan of Cooking. Far from it! Many of you will find my child-oriented meals pretty boring. *You* have to decide how you want to organize, shop, and cook for *your* family. *Eat Healthy* will give you the information and the tools needed to individualize your strategies, improve the quality of your food, and still save a fortune.

My book will show you ways to cut costs on nearly every food item you buy—from fresh produce to chicken breasts to whole grains. And if you're looking for overall strategies to help you save big, you'll find a crash course explaining bulk buying, couponing, refunding, cooperatives, bartering, getting organized, meal-planning, mega-cooking®, making or cooking your own food, gardening, preserving food, government programs, and more. Chapters Two and Three tell you how to "beat the system," whether you do so at the store or elsewhere. The section on Resources provides valuable information, addresses, and phone numbers to get you started.

Perhaps you've read all the theories behind saving on good food, but can't understand how to really make it happen. You'll find help in Chapter Four, where a hypothetical family changes their lifestyle little by little, one or two changes a week, for 52 weeks of the year. The results are big savings on their food budget, and a healthier way of eating as well.

You may think you have a good excuse—from catering to demanding children to having very little time to cook—for spending lots of money on high-cost, low-nutrition convenience foods at the supermarket. If so, refer to Chapter Five. There may be an answer there for you. Or look over the point-by-point checklist in Chapter Seven for quick, excellent ideas to help you save money on healthy groceries.

Are you wondering if all this—whatever you decide to do—requires an incredible amount of time and energy? Not nearly as much as you might think. It takes me about 15 minutes to devise a shopping list based on store specials, and about two hours to shop with my four children—Eric, 9; Christian, 8; Lisa, 6; and Mary, 4—in tow. I enjoy cooking, but between home-schooling my three oldest, running a household, and writing, I average less than an hour a day preparing food. You'll find my recipes in Chapter Six to be mostly fast and easy, as well as healthy, dishes. Your family will like them, too.

All in all, I think I have some wonderfully helpful advice to share. I know there are many, many people who can benefit from the information in *Eat Healthy for $50 a Week*. Perhaps you're living from paycheck to paycheck, laid off, unemployed, or trying to survive on Social Security. Maybe you're a working parent who yearns to stay home with your children. You might need extra cash for a son or daughter's college education, or a nicer home, or other dreams in your life. In addition, maybe you're now on a low-cholesterol diet, overweight, or concerned about possible heart disease or cancer. If so, I have good news: you can outline a very healthy diet for yourself and your family, and you can do it for very little money.

In fact, the grocery budget is a perfect place to start saving dollars. While it may not be possible to cut back immediately on house or car payments or other expenses, you can begin to economize on good food *today*. If you are a typical American family spending, say, $120 a week, scaling down to $50 is a $70 weekly savings, a $280 monthly savings, and a $3,640 yearly savings, all of it tax-free "income." That's a lot of cash.

So with all this said, why not begin to *Eat Healthy for $50 a Week*?

CHAPTER 1

Real-Life Shopping

Have you ever made a quick stop at the grocery store for milk and bread, and found yourself filling your cart—and emptying your pocketbook—instead? Of course you have; we all have. And that's how I used to do most of my shopping. I enjoyed rambling through the supermarket, choosing a few essential items, and splurging on anything else that looked appealing. When we implemented our $50-a-week food budget, I simply couldn't do that anymore. Fifty dollars plus impulse buying yielded two and a half bags of groceries, much of it items that were not even very nutritious! That was certainly not enough to feed a family of six well for a week.

Three years ago, I faced another challenge in trying to buy healthier foods. How could I increase our fruit and vegetable consumption without spending a fortune? Where could I get the best buys on whole grain bread, canola oil, chicken? Which was cheaper, a cooperative or a local grocery store?

I've had to take my own advice and thoroughly re-research bulk buying, couponing, refunding, co-ops, bartering, gardening, gleaning and other strategies mentioned in this and the next two chapters. Still, most of my shopping is done at local stores. Here are the guidelines I decided on nearly six years ago (I still find them very helpful).

1. *Set a limit on spending.*
It's been my experience that if I allow myself $75, I spend that much just as easily as I spend $50. Restricting my outlay helps me to

think creatively about possibilities. I have to carefully examine priorities. Do I really need to buy juice boxes for the children, or expensive snack crackers? Is there a cheaper, healthier substitute? What helps most is thinking of the budget as an adventure rather than a toilsome burden. How much can I buy for $50?—this is my objective. It's a kind of game to try and get more for my money each week.

Nobody says you should spend what I spend. You may actually have to go lower, or you may find $75 to $100 a much more comfortable range. Limiting yourself is still important. It makes you feel in control of your budget and forces you to use money wisely.

2. *Compare prices.*

I have about 100 prices from my favorite store memorized, not because I planned to, but just because I'm interested. You don't need to do this, of course; it's easier and more helpful to keep a "price book" with the cost of items you buy regularly. For example, your notebook might look something like this:

Store	12 oz. orange juice		1 loaf whole wheat bread		16 oz. frozen peas	
National	Name brand	1.39	Name brand	1.29	Name brand	1.69
	Store brand	1.19	Store brand	.99	Store brand	1.29
	Generic	.89	Generic	.79	Generic none	
A&P	Name brand	1.29	Name brand	1.39	Name brand	1.49
	Store brand	.99	Store brand	.89	Store brand none	
	Generic	.79	Generic none		Generic	1.39

On the line above, across from National, I have recorded brand name prices. Line two is store brand prices, and line three, generic. To compile the information for your price book, you can do all your shopping at National one week and quickly jot down prices as you buy. Next week do the same at A&P, and so on until you've completed a list for several stores. The store with the overall lowest prices will be your new base store.

Supermarkets are only one possibility. I have checked out—and continue to check out—discount and wholesale grocers, food co-ops, day-old bakeries, produce stands, farmers' markets, dairies, buying clubs, cheese factory outlets, meat markets, scratch-and-dent outlets, and health food stores. In the past few months, I've been buying most of my spices from Olde Town Spice Shoppe in a historic district near my home. We've even found cheap tomatoes, in season, at a florist's! You never know where you'll uncover a bargain.

To research possibilities, you might want to start with your telephone company's Yellow Pages under Grocers and/or Food. Even if you live in a rural area, I think you'll be surprised at what you may find in your phone book. Also talk to friends and neighbors about good buys in your area, wherever you live. I've gotten some great leads just by asking around.

3. *Buy most groceries from the cheapest store.*

This may seem so obvious it's hardly worth mentioning. It's surprising, though, how many people will only shop someplace that offers them spotlessly waxed floors and calculators on the carts. I understand. But such stores are usually not the places where you'll save the most money.

My personal favorite is Aldi, a no-frills discount warehouse that offers a limited selection, but at about 50 percent below most supermarket prices.[1] It's amazing how much cheaper some stores are than others. Many products at Aldi, for example, cost less than supermarket brand names advertising a half-price savings! In other words, when a local supermarket's "special" on wheat bran cereal is $1.69, Aldi's store brand price is $1.29 (with little, if any, difference in quality). This is why it is so important to price check by referring to your notebook, then select a store that offers the best deals.

4. *Supplement by shopping at other stores whose weekly specials are outstanding, or use alternative strategies.*

Did you know that supermarkets sometimes take a loss on a few items in order to entice you to buy there? "Loss-leader" specials—some or all of those advertised on the front and back of weekly fliers—may actually be priced below a store's cost. You can easily spot the real bargains by quickly leafing through several ads, price notebook in hand. It takes me about five minutes to decide on my second store for the week (if I go to one) based on the items that I need that are on sale. In another 10 minutes, I've combed through that store's ad a second time and have my shopping list written.

I won't say it's easy, but I often stop at three or more stores a week. All three are generally within a five-mile radius of my home, and bargains have to be incredible to lure me farther away. The children and I usually swing by the produce stand first. Next we might shop at a supermarket, then Aldi. The penny candy store is only two doors down from Aldi. Even with Eric, Christian, Lisa, and Mary trailing along and helping(?), our entire excursion takes about two hours from start to finish.

In the last three years, I've begun to use several other alternative strategies instead of shopping at another store for specials. I make much of my own bread now, and Michael and I are trying to garden again this summer. (More on these strategies, and dozens of others, in the next two chapters.)

5. *Make a detailed shopping list.*

As I write down items I need for the week, I match up ideas for meals with store specials. If fish is on sale, for example, I buy and serve that instead of chicken. Our menus are flexible so that I can take advantage of cheaper foods.

My shopping list starts with essentials, and then I add other food I would also like to buy. I estimate the total cost for everything on my list. If I'm under $50 I can add more; if over, I have to delete a few items and rethink my meal plans. Sometimes I take a little extra money with me just in case. But most days I'm within a dollar or two of my estimate.

Substitutions are justified when I find an unexpected good deal. Aldi sometimes has surprise specials, like overly ripe bananas for 10 cents a pound, or "buy one, get one free" loaves of whole wheat bread. When I find a bargain like one of these, I cross some long-term baking items off my list and stock up as much as I can.

But in order to demonstrate just how my system works, I want to share an actual shopping list and menu plans for five consecutive days. I usually shop on Tuesday or Wednesday, so I recorded both the items I bought and how I used them throughout the following calendar week. You'll also find a record of my next three shopping lists and 16 consecutive days of menus in Appendix One. Below, I'll detail the list and total prices, then explain why I bought what I did. (Items are arranged in approximate categories as I knew I needed them.) Menu plans follow.

SHOPPING LIST

Week 1

From Aldi

3 gallons ½% milk	1 13-ounce box animal crackers
1 pound part-skim mozzarella cheese	1 pound graham crackers
	3 loaves whole wheat bread
2 dozen eggs	2 pounds brown sugar

2 8-ounce containers raspberry yogurt
2 packages (10 each large) tortillas
2 9-ounce bags of pretzels
1 8-ounce bag tortilla chips
1 15-ounce box fruit rings cereal
1 6-ounce can water-packed tuna
1 small package taco seasoning
1 4-ounce can mushrooms
1 head cauliflower
1 pound frozen peas
5 quarts ice cream

Total: $41.62

4 pounds white sugar
5 pounds white flour
1 13-ounce box crisp rice cereal
1 18-ounce box corn flakes
1 15-ounce can salmon
1 small box macaroni and cheese
1 20-ounce can pineapple
1 pound carrots
6 pounds apples
1 pound frozen corn
1 24-ounce container lemonade mix
2 12-ounce cans frozen orange juice

From Vaccaro & Sons Produce
7 oranges
1 pound grapes
18 bananas
10 pounds red potatoes
1 head cabbage

Total: $6.08

From Ben Franklin
60 penny candies

Total: $.62

Grand Total: $48.32

As you can see from my list, I buy a lot of what you probably buy. Most of my groceries came from Aldi, as usual. The produce stand is less than a mile farther down the road. Two weeks before, I had ordered several items from a cooperative and stocked up on brown rice, canola oil, and low-fat cheddar cheese. I went over budget that time, but am under budget for the next three lists; my *average* is still $50 a week.

At first glance, some of the foods on my list—such as eggs, ice cream, and the macaroni and cheese dinner—may appear to be high in fat. To accommodate the children's nutritional needs, I do feed them a slightly higher-fat diet than my husband, Michael, and I eat. Eric and Christian enjoy scrambled, whole eggs two mornings a week (the girls don't like them). But in nearly all the baking I do for the family, I use only egg whites and very little fat. In the same way, the children eat most of the ice cream—though Aldi's brand has 6 grams of fat per serving, not as high as some brands—two or three times a week. We grown-ups have small portions. Also, in the next three weeks of menus, you'll notice that I bought *low-fat* ice cream and sherbert, because I wanted some, too! (See Appendix.)

The macaroni and cheese dinner deserves special mention, as this is a good example of a traditionally high-fat food that can easily be converted to low-fat. The contents of the box itself, before preparation, contain 1 gram of fat (2 percent of a 2,000 calorie diet) per serving. When ¼ cup margarine and ¼ cup 2 percent milk are added, fat content jumps to 26 percent, including 15 percent saturated fat! However, I've learned to omit the margarine completely and use nonfat dry milk. This keeps both fat content and cost per serving very low. And the children like it!

We have also converted over to lower-fat "snack foods"—no more potato chips! The children do have tortilla chips once or twice a week. But we usually serve animal crackers (3 grams of fat per serving), graham crackers (4 grams), pretzels (1.5 grams), or other low-fat alternatives. I'm trying to do more baking as well: homemade breads are often both cheaper and healthier.

Prepackaged cereal is low in fat, though I have to admit that a box of fruit rings has its sugar. This sugary cereal is our once-a-week breakfast indulgence. We also buy penny candies at a store just two doors down from Aldi; these are *tiny* pieces, but 15 of them in each of my children's hands seem like vast bounty to them, even though 15 total the size of one regular candy bar! Each child eats three pieces as a low-fat lunch dessert.

Perhaps you noticed that my shopping list does not include any non-food items, such as aluminum foil, paper towels, or laundry detergent. I generally buy those twice a month. We try to make do with reusable goods whenever possible. I even recycle some very carefully-washed foil and plastic bags. I have not recorded anything other than food, but even with these items figured in, my average weekly grocery bill is still $55 to $60.

Here are the menus for breakfast, lunch, dinners, and two daily snacks—real-life menus, remember!—that followed from my shopping.

ONE WEEK'S MENUS
(following Wednesday's shopping)

Thursday

B: Cold cereal with milk
S: Bananas (and later) carrot sticks
L: Peanut butter and jelly sandwiches on whole wheat bread, yogurt, pretzels, 3 penny candies, milk
S: Watermelon or oranges
D: Spaghetti*, garlic breadsticks*, lettuce salad, cauliflower "trees," low-fat pudding cake, water or tea

Friday

B: Oatmeal, whole wheat toast, scrambled eggs, milk
S: Frozen fruit popsicles*
L: Enchiladas* with mozzarella cheese and salsa, graham crackers, fruit roll-ups, 3 penny candies, milk
S: Choice of apples, bananas, or grapes
D: Roast beef, baked potatoes and gravy*, green beans, homemade oatmeal bread, ice cream, water or tea

Saturday

B: Whole wheat oatmeal pancakes*, milk
S: Frozen fruit popsicles* (and later) carrot sticks
L: Macaroni and cheese*, pretzels, applesauce, milk
S: Homemade whole wheat French bread* (fresh from the oven!)
D: Lasagna*, French bread*, veggie tray with lettuce wedges, cauliflower, green peppers, tomatoes, and carrots, breadsticks*, cinnamon custard pie (see Five-Minute Chocolate Custard Pie)*, lemonade*

Sunday

B: Cold cereal with milk
S: Pretzels
L: Lunch out (we ate lots of fruit from a brunch bar)

S: Frozen fruit popsicles*
D: Leftovers veggies—carrots, green peppers, and cauliflower—with nonfat dip, French bread*, watermelon slices, milk

Monday

B: Whole wheat oatmeal pancakes*, milk
S: Grapes and sliced bananas
L: Low-fat cheddar cheese and crackers, alfalfa sprouts* and nonfat dip, yogurt, 3 penny candies, milk
S: Watermelon slices
D: Baked (skinless) chicken, low-fat whole grain stuffing* and low-fat gravy*, corn on the cob, eggplant*, ice cream, water or tea

Our food is pretty basic, as you can see. We eat few casseroles and soups because no one in the family likes casseroles, and Michael is the only one who really enjoys soup. (I do keep trying new soup recipes, though, because I know how good it is for you.) Although we serve meat nearly every day for dinner, our per-serving size is generally only a few ounces. Instead we offer large portions of whole grain breads, pasta, brown rice, and vegetables.

As mentioned earlier, I make it a point to see that Eric, Christian, Lisa, and Mary have at least three one-cup servings of milk or milk products, one generous serving of vitamin C and a mixture of five fruits and vegetables every day (well, OK, almost every day!). This may not seem obvious when reading through the menus. For example, on Cereal Days—the most popular breakfasts of the week, I might add—the children are allowed three bowls of cereal, getting at least two milk servings each, first thing in the morning. Sometimes, instead of orange juice, we spread out the vitamin C in watermelon, tomatoes, oranges, broccoli, potatoes, etc. throughout the day. Eric, my very-tall-and-growing-fast boy, often has two fruits per snack, and Mary has one whole, large fruit, double servings for each of them at one snack time.

I eat almost everything the children eat, including popsicles, right along with them: with all I do, I *need* the energy boost. Michael's more likely to skip the snacks and eat his "five a day"—and other

*Starred items can be found in Recipes. Look them up; you'll be surprised at the low-fat content!

good food—at meal times. The children and I drink orange juice at most dinner meals now, though at the time I recorded the menus, we were usually having ice water (or occasional Kool-Aid for the kids) and/or iced tea.

This week we had plenty of vegetables. Michael visited some out-of-town friends, who loaded him down with a big sackful of tomatoes, cucumbers, zucchini, eggplant, and a cabbage. My brother and sister-in-law spent the night with us, and brought along a huge watermelon. I shared some of the veggies with our neighbors. Later, I bartered a zucchini for some vinegar when I ran out!

As you can imagine, I cook fairly large quantities, and we often have leftovers. I use up everything in the refrigerator, and start all over again, every two to three days. Sometimes we grown-ups have leftovers for lunch, sometimes I serve them "straight" or recycled at dinner, and sometimes I freeze whatever is left.

We've all made a major sacrifice in occasionally giving up nightly desserts. I hope to improve our record to occasional *dessert* rather than occasional *going without*. I am certain we could save money if we skipped the sugary finale to our meals, but it's not something we're willing to give up just yet. Instead, we've converted to low-fat and/or more nutritious desserts.

You may not agree with this, but it's my personal theory that asking children (and maybe grown-ups) to give up sugar completely causes them to crave it and eventually overindulge. That's why we allow limited amounts of low-fat candies for lunchtime treats. Overall, though, we eat less sugar now than we did two years ago.

Remember, I promised *real-life* menus. It was very tempting to doctor these listings and show you perfectly balanced meals. Unfortunately, I don't always succeed in feeding us perfectly! At one point, I considered recording menus as I *planned* to serve them, a model for the month, so to speak. But I thought it might be more helpful to play "true confessions" and tell you what we *really* ate for three weeks.

I am not trying to justify my menus nor insist that you try to follow them. Not at all. These listings are here to give you an idea of exactly what I do and do not serve within the restraints of my $50 budget. I know you'll want to plan your own system, your own menus, and your own recipes to help your family eat healthy and inexpensively. Turn to the next chapter for some surefire strategies to save money on nutritious food.

NOTES:

1. As of this writing, Aldi is primarily located in midwestern states, but the company is rapidly expanding eastward. See Resources for a complete listing of current divisional headquarters' phone numbers. Save-a-Lot Food Stores, comparable to Aldi, are available in some states (including southern ones) where Aldi is not. See Resources. To the best of my knowledge, there is nothing comparable to Aldi and Save-A-Lot in much of the western U.S. and some other parts of the country. Those of you who live in these areas may have to try alternative strategies, such as shopping warehouse membership clubs or cooperatives, to find the best deals.

CHAPTER 2

Beat the System at the Store

A few years ago I really didn't know much about saving money on food. Since then, I've discovered ways to "beat the supermarket system" through careful buying of loss-leader sale items, marked-down meat and produce, and day-old bread. I've also learned more about bulk buying at warehouse stores, large-scale couponing, refunding, and other smart shopping principles. Today, I get a lot more for my money than I used to!

As I mentioned in the last chapter, there are all sorts of retail and wholesale outlets—grocery stores, markets, buying clubs, warehouses, scratch-and-dent stores, etc.—where you can purchase low-cost groceries. The trick is to beat the system at that particular store.

SAVE MONEY ON WHAT YOU BUY

Let's assume that you've already chosen a base store and are ready to do some serious shopping. Before you even begin, beware of "supermarket (or warehouse store, etc.) seduction." You know what I mean: aisle upon aisle of luscious-looking convenience foods, perfectly arranged, a real temptation for your senses. Keep in mind that grocery stores ordinarily make only a narrow profit margin on most foods. Stores rake in the most money from items like potato chips, deli items, and non-food goods (cosmetics, for example). There's nothing wrong with the supermarket employing please-put-me-in-your-cart strategies, but there's also no reason why *you* have to buy into the seduction.

So take your list along and stick to it. Go to the store well rested (if you can). Buy generic, slightly damaged, marked-down or store-brand groceries whenever possible. Try to purchase large quantities in order to drop per-ounce costs. And above all, keep in mind *why* you're doing this: you have better things to do with the money you're *not* spending on food!

That said, here are some guidelines for saving money on specific foods.

Meats

Watch carefully for sales and stock up on the feature of the week. Buy a month's worth of chicken at 39 cents a pound, and next week a month's worth of beef roast for half price. Some supermarkets feature family packs, with quantity meat offered at a discount.

When turkeys and hams go on sale during Thanksgiving and Christmas, try to have enough money set aside to invest in more than one for your freezer. Later, you can substitute turkey for chicken in all your chicken recipes.

Purchase whole chickens and cut them up yourself: all you need is a very sharp knife and a standard cookbook's directions. If you cut, skin, and bone your own chicken breasts, you'll probably spend about 50 cents a pound and less for these "gourmet pieces," the ones that ordinarily fetch $3 a pound and more! You can also bag and freeze like pieces—all wings, or legs, for example—for use in future meals.

Consider buying meat in quantity. You may be able to purchase half a side of beef at the meat market for a price 50 percent less than the supermarket's. Find a few friends with freezer space, and you're all set.

Buy fish or seafood that is currently in season.

Rely on cheaper turkey or chicken cold cuts and hot dogs rather than those made from beef and pork.

Ask meat managers if they offer discounts on the ends of deli meats or mark down overbuys. I have located one local store that sells surplus meat at half price, and less.

Negotiate directly with the meat manager when you plan to buy large quantities of meat. My friend Jill, who prepares six months' worth of meals at a time, often does so and saves considerably.

Cost compare, and you may be able to buy on-sale meat butcher. If so, ask him to give you the bones and other throwaway along with the prime cuts; you can make them into soups and broths.

Dairy Foods

Purchasing milk products at the supermarket can be expensive, but there are other options. You may have to shop around to find the best prices. Start with a food warehouse or buyers' club, Aldi, Save-A-Lot, or similar store. Can you locate a dairy or cheese outlet through your local Yellow Pages? Even driving some distance for milk products may be worth a once-a-month trip, especially if you buy in large quantities and freeze milk and cheese.

Buy "ends" of cheese rolls at the deli section; some supermarkets mark these down in price.

Sometimes grated cheese sold by the pound at in-store salad bars, may be cheaper than cheese in the dairy section.[1]

Many dairy foods—milk substitutes, soft margarine, low-fat sour cream, whipped topping, yogurt, and even yogurt cheese—can be made cheaply from scratch. See the Recipe Index for ideas.

Produce

As a rule, don't buy fresh fruits and vegetables at the supermarket unless you can find them as "loss leaders." Keep your eyes open and you should be able to locate a produce stand in your area, one that stays open year round. I used to frequent a stand where "loose" grapes and slightly bruised apples were sold at 75 percent off the regular low prices. Sometimes such bargains are not readily apparent, so you should be inquisitive.

Wherever you shop, purchase only what's in season and/or on sale. Apples, of course, are common in the fall, as are pumpkins and winter squash. Oranges and grapefruits peak in November through April. Strawberries are best in late spring. See the chart in the back for detailed information.

Wherever you shop, ask the produce manager if he or she would be willing to set out bags of "browner" bananas at half price. Find out what he or she does with damaged produce and volunteer to buy it cheap (or better yet, haul it off for free).

Weigh bagged produce to find the one that's slightly heavier. You may discover a two-pound bag, for example, that holds two and a half pounds of carrots.

Try to process older and damaged produce immediately for maximum nutrition and minimum waste. If leafy vegetables are wilted, pick off the brown edges, sprinkle with cool water, wrap in a towel, and refrigerate. You can freeze most fruits and vegetables in airtight containers or freezer bags; consult a standard cookbook for more specific advice.

Fresh produce is best for you, and the fresher the better. Canned fruits and vegetables have less nutritional value and a higher sodium content than frozen or fresh equivalents. But if you must rely on canned produce, look for store brand, generic, or on-sale name brands whenever possible. Those who cook in large quantities should consider buying institutional size cans of vegetables, which are often much cheaper per ounce than their smaller counterparts. Another alternative is to purchase generic frozen vegetables, then steam them in a covered saucepan; the cost will probably be higher, but so will the vitamin content.

Breads, Grains, Pasta, Cereals

I used to buy all my bread from a day-old bakery, saving about 50 percent over supermarket prices. Now I purchase fresh whole wheat loaves at Aldi for even less than that. Compare prices carefully in your area to find the best, low-cost source.

If you do purchase day-old breads, try to stock up on varieties that can be easily reheated. Slightly tough rolls, for example, taste delicious when oven-browned until crispy. Or try my mother-in-law's trick: she heats water in a large pan on the stove, adds a wire basket filled with day-old bread, and steams the bread briefly until hot and tender.

Buy whole grains and grind them yourself in a mill. See Appendix Three for more information.

Bulk buy whole grain products, like oats and cornmeal; baking supplies like flour and yeast; as well as beans, brown rice, and pasta. (You may want to freeze grains overnight, then seal in airtight containers.) Check the bulk-buy section of your supermarket. Or go to a warehouse store!

BULK BUY FROM WAREHOUSE STORES

Recently Michael and I were given a free membership in a wholesale club just down the road. Sam's Club has good prices and good quality. So we tried stocking up on, among other things, Captain Crunch cereal and tortilla chips.

It was fun while it lasted. The only trouble was, it didn't last as long as it was supposed to. For us, buying ten times our normal amount of chips did *not* mean we had chips ten times as long. It meant we ate a lot more a lot faster. Our problem with buying in bulk is that we tend to eat in bulk, too.

It is not this way for everyone. I know of some families who visit the wholesale club, stock-up stores, and other outlets once a month, buy wisely, and then consume wisely. Stocking up on items such as yeast, for example, makes sense: it stays tucked away in the refrigerator, and you can't sit down in front of the TV and overindulge in it. Jackie Iglehart (publisher of *The Penny Pincher*) purchases bulk flour from a bakery owner, and so is able to make homemade bread for pennies a loaf. Smart bulk buying like this amounts to huge savings.

Mike Yorkey, in his excellent book, *Saving Money Any Way You Can,* interviewed an anonymous warehouse club insider for insight into how these clubs work. Most surprising to me was "Paul's" explanation that his own company, Price Club[2], makes *no* money on merchandise, selling goods at cost. As Paul says, "If it weren't for the annual membership fees, we couldn't stay in business." Prices are obviously good: what you have to determine, as a smart consumer, is this: will I save enough money buying at the club this year to justify the cost of membership? In certain parts of the country, you probably will, in others, perhaps not.

When and if you shop at warehouse clubs, follow this advice from *The Frugal Times:*[3]

- Don't buy products just to try out at home. Make sure you really like and will use the product.
- Don't buy products you can get cheaper elsewhere.
- Don't buy products that supposedly save you money if you're spending more in the long run by buying more (e.g., my tortilla chips story).
- Don't buy margarine, canned vegetables, meats, standard sodas, and bread at the warehouse, as you can usually find them at cost or below at supermarkets, especially with use of double coupons.
- Do look around on your first visit. Note prices, unit costs, and quantities before you buy.

- Do go at a time that's less hectic than rush hour.
- Do make a list and stick to it. Don't allow yourself to linger and be tempted.
- Do buy just enough to last until your next visit. In the meantime, you will probably be able to use other shopping strategies that might save you more money.

Paul (the anonymous Price Club man) adds some insider tips: "Get to know some of the staff. They can tell you about the hot bargains or when something new is expected to arrive. They'll know which slow-movers have been marked down, or when price changes are made."[4]

Paul also details Price Club's elaborate merchandise coding system; your local warehouse store probably uses a similar system, and personnel there could explain it to you. *Ask* about good buys. I did, and was referred to a damaged goods section at Sam's Club by a helpful clerk.

One more word on bulk buying from stores: try to keep extra money set aside for the best bargains. Check stores regularly for damaged goods and loss-leader items. Buy as much as you can possibly afford when the price is right.

TRY "THE PANTRY PRINCIPLE™"

Barbara Salsbury, a nationally recognized consumer specialist, sent me her video called *Beating the High Cost of Eating*. I was impressed with Barbara's research and presentation: this woman is a true expert when it comes to giving advice on the best strategies to use when shopping at stores.

Barbara tells the inside story of how supermarkets excel at "supermarketing," doing all they can to convince you to buy plenty of food you really don't need (as well as food you do need) at premium prices. Her video shares several REVERSE KEYS™[5] designed to help you shop much more economically.

One of the most interesting concepts Barbara shares is THE PANTRY PRINCIPLE™, her strategy of keeping the pantry continually well stocked through careful buying. Here's how it works, in Barbara's own words.

"The habit of stocking up on items when the price is right yields constant savings. Even if you have to put off buying a few nonessential items . . . use the money you would have spent on them to establish the routine of stocking up when those prices are right. For example: If you know you use canned pineapple about twice a month, plan to buy a case or half case when the case lot sales are scheduled. You won't need to buy pineapple again for several weeks or perhaps several months, or until you see it at a price you are willing to pay. Next shopping trip your list will not have to include these 'stocked-up' items—which in turn gives you more buying power to follow the same strategy again! The bargains, benefits, and buying power will begin to compound! Taking into account your space, budget, and storage life of the items on sale, stock up on groceries and other items you consistently use when they are at rock-bottom prices. If you are shrewd you can start buying items only when they are at the best prices and never pay full price for them again!"[5]

Using THE PANTRY PRINCIPLE™—and the shopping advice that goes with it—is certainly one valid way to save money on food. This is especially helpful information for those of you who live in an area with no Aldi or Save-a-Lot stores. See Resources.

USE COUPONS

Maybe you're looking for additional ways to save money at the super-market. If so, large-scale couponing and/or refunding may be the answer for you.

Cheapskate Monthly newsletter featured a woman who claims to have "saved solely with coupons and refunds a total of . . . *$17,433.-17*" since 1980! Twice a week, Mary Ann Maring spends at least an hour scanning the ads for local supermarkets, clipping store coupons and determining the best buys for what she needs. Next she goes through her extensive files, matching up manufacturers' coupons with sales and store coupons wherever possible. To keep current, Mary Ann purges her files every four months. Expired coupons are pitched, and soon-to-expire ones are rotated to the front of each category.

Needless to say, $17,000 is a lot of money. I found Mary Ann's approach intriguing: she has learned to play the couponing game to great personal advantage. As *Cheapskate Monthly* notes, "There were many items for which she would pay only a few cents and occasionally she pointed out an item she would be getting absolutely *free!*"

Once in a while I do use coupons. Recently at the supermarket I picked up two candy bars for five cents each, five cans of name-brand vegetables for 60 cents total, and two bottles of Softsoap for 60 cents each. I know couponing works. But I must admit I don't think, generally speaking, it merits a significant investment of my time.

For example, by using coupons the Del Monte vegetables cost 15 cents a can. The same size private-label corn is 25 cents a can at my base store, Aldi. I honestly can't tell a difference in taste. And to save 10 cents a can, I had to find a store featuring Del Monte vegetables on sale, clip a coupon, search the shelves a few moments to find an exact match, and redeem a double coupon. Maybe I dislike all of this bother because of four children hurrying me along. I want things quick and easy, and the extra work for ten pennies is simply not worth it to me.

And here's another problem. Most coupons are printed for highly packaged convenience foods, like expensive, ready-to-eat cereal or salad dressings. So even if I buy on sale with double coupons, I may still pay more for an item that I can make myself.

Recently at the grocery store, I did a cost comparison of three items at original price and after double coupons, contrasting with both a name brand and Aldi's brand. (I assume you could find similar prices at a warehouse store in your area.) Here's what I discovered:

Lucky Charms cereal costs $3.69; with a 50-cent coupon doubled, $2.69. But I can buy a similar product, same size, at Aldi for $1.69. Or I can serve my entire family oatmeal for breakfast for less than 50 cents!

Yoplait yogurt costs 69 cents; with a "30 cents off 2" coupon doubled, 39 cents each; at Aldi, yogurt is 29 cents for the same size; and homemade, at about 15 cents, is even cheaper.

Log Cabin Syrup costs $3.29; with a 40-cent coupon doubled, $2.49; Aldi's version is 79 cents for a smaller size, or $1.58 for two equaling the Log Cabin bottle; and homemade costs 80 cents or less.

If saving money is your main goal, you would have to locate these items on sale and double a coupon to even approach the cost of the homemade products. This is possible, especially when making use of what serious couponers call single, double, and triple plays, and grand slams. Mike Yorkey describes how it works:

"The simplest transaction is a 'single play,' which takes place when a consumer uses a standard cents-off coupon, such as a straight fifty cents off a box of Rice Krispies.

"But you can do more. . . . Let's say your local supermarket is having a buy-one, get-one-free sale on Ragu spaghetti sauce. The cost of each jar is $1.77. You pull two jars of Ragu off the shelf and take two Ragu coupons out of your file box. If you have two coupons for fifty cents off, that's a double play. Final cost: 77 cents.

"But if you're shopping in a supermarket that doubles coupons, you can go for a 'triple play!' Again, you pull two jars of Ragu off the shelf for $1.77. Then, you take two Ragu coupons out of your file box. Each doubled, fifty-cent coupon is worth one dollar each, for a total of two dollars. Because you paid $1.77 for the two jars but received two dollars at the checkout stand, the supermarket just paid *you* 23 cents to purchase two jars of Ragu. . . .

"The ultimate coupon play is a 'grand slam.' That's when you have manufacturers' coupons *and* store coupons (found in newspaper inserts) in your file box. Let's say the store is again offering the two-for-one deal on Ragu sauce. In your hot little hands, you're holding two fifty-cent manufacturer's coupons, which when doubled equals two dollars off. But the supermarket also has in-store coupons for twenty-five cents off, which double to fifty cents each for a total of one dollar. In all, you receive a $3 refund, which means the grocer just paid you $1.23 to put two jars of Ragu into your cart."[6]

Yes, believe it or not, this is legal. And though the work involved may be mind-boggling, there is a certain thrill in achieving a "grand slam."

Couponing may be a viable option for you if you think of it as a hobby, enjoy name-brand products, or have a difficult time finding discounted food. Here are some recommendations for novices from Jackie Iglehart of *The Penny Pincher* newsletter, and Mary Kenyon, an expert couponer:

- Subscribe to the Sunday newspaper, a great source of coupons. Also check the food section of the daily paper, women's magazines, and boxes at the front of some supermarkets.
- Ask willing friends and relatives to save coupons for you. Consider setting up a coupon exchange box at the library.
- Look over couponing magazines (see Resources under "Refunding") to decide whether a subscription is worth your while.
- Clip all coupons and file them in appropriate categories, such as Breads, Meats, and Frozen Foods.
- Make a coupon file from a small box, tabbed and divided by

cardboard pieces. Always take your coupon box along when you leave home.

- Decide ahead of time what coupons you will use at the store, and transfer them to an envelope. Arrange the coupons in the order that you find foods placed in store aisles, on your usual route or alphabetically.
- Don't buy items just because you have a coupon unless it's something you'd use anyway, or unless it's free or nearly free.
- Besides buying on sale, try to use coupons for products that you find in damaged or discontinued bins.
- Stockpile when you find a particularly good deal.
- Take advantage of rain checks. If a store is out of a sale product for which you have coupons, ask Customer Service to give you a "voucher" that can be redeemed at a later time.

Cheapskate Monthly suggests you may be an excellent candidate for couponing if you like to organize things, have tenacity and patience, can see the big picture, are flexible, and enjoy a challenge.

But if you're thinking, as I am, that this is just too much work, then large-scale couponing may not be for you. Says Amy Dacyczyn, author of *The Tightwad Gazette*, "I feel that using couponing and refunding as your major grocery strategy will reduce your food bill, but not as much as if you use a combination of strategies." In the end, it comes down to personal preference.

DO REFUNDING

Some of us have taken advantage of a refund offer or two. Perhaps we've dutifully clipped the UPC symbol from a box of cereal, mailed it in, and received a check for $1 in the mail. I never found myself too enthusiastic about a return of a couple of bucks a month, especially considering the work and postage involved. Then again, there *are* ways to use refunding as a major means of saving money on groceries.

The Tightwad Gazette describes Mary Kenyon of Independence, Iowa, who spends about $385 monthly to feed a family of six. What's remarkable about it? Well, Mary saves an average of 20 percent of that amount through coupon use, and receives back *$110* each month on refunds, even after postage! That brings her weekly grocery bill down to $50.

I gave Mary a call to learn more. She tells me that she is now saving almost 30 percent off the cost of food through couponing. But what I really wanted to know about was refunding: exactly how does one get back all that money? Mary wrote:

"I save all my labels, receipts, and UPC symbols and file them in Ziploc bags according to product categories (i.e., juice, aspirin, cereal, crackers). I have two file cabinets and shelves with boxes to hold my qualifiers. I have several traders (other refunders) who I regularly trade refund forms and complete deals with. This way I am able to take advantage of many more refunds that are put out by manufacturers each month. . . . I spend 15–20 hours a week working on refunding, in 15-minute to half-hour stretches. This includes clipping and sorting coupons, planning a grocery list, cutting and filing qualifiers, sending out for refunds, and organizing trades."

What does all this effort get Mary? "I provide 85 percent of my children's Christmas gifts through my refunding," Mary explained. "I usually have extra T-shirts and watches to give to my brothers and have also given baskets of trial-size products and food products I've gotten free with coupons to my mother, a sister, or an elderly shut-in." In addition, "After postage ($15 to $20 a month), I average $90 in cash, another $25 to $35 in free product coupons, and five to 20 free gifts back. If you subtract that $90 in cash from what I spent on groceries, then I really did save a great deal."

Michele Easter, publisher of *Refunding Makes Cents! (RMC)*, says, "I receive many checks in the mail *every month* by taking the time to peel labels, cut off UPCs, and mail away for cash, gifts, and free coupons. I mail for at least 100 refunds every month on all types of household products. So my mailbox is stuffed with checks for $1, $5, $10, and more, and I receive free T-shirts, toys, tapes, etc., plus wonderful coupons for free full-size products."

I scanned the pages of a recent issue of *RMC,* and was impressed with both the scope and complexity of the bulletin. But I must confess I still have my doubts about refunding. For example, here is a typical offer:

"Ten free jars of Gerber 1st, 2nd or 3rd Foods Baby Foods. Send 48 UPCs from Gerber baby foods or juices." Forty-eight jars of baby food, at an average price of 50 cents each, adds up to $24. You get ten free jars and so supposedly save $5. It all sounds impressive until you consider that 48 meals of a homemade equivalent, whipped up in the blender from your own delicious food, would only cost a few dollars or less. Which makes more sense, to not spend much money in the first place, or to spend a fair amount, then work at least an hour to get some back? Refunders claim big savings, but for my family, most of the time, it doesn't make cents *or* sense.

Here's another offer listed in *RMC:*

"Free mermaid doll. Send five UPCs from Chicken of the Sea products for a free doll. . . ." Oh yes, and there *is* a $1.95 postage and handling fee. So I buy five cans of name-brand tuna at 89 cents each (the cheapest Chicken of the Sea product I could find), add p&h and arrive at a figure of $6.40 needed for my "free" doll. Wouldn't it be simpler, and much cheaper, to buy generic tuna at 49 cents a can? And pick up a mermaid doll—as we did—at a garage sale for a quarter? My total cost for five cans of tuna *and* a doll is $2.70. Who's really saving money here, not to mention time?

Refunders will argue that it's not that simple, and their lengthy newsletters bear witness to that. One way to make money through refunding, for example, is to trade forms that you already have to someone who doesn't have them. Currently, there is controversy concerning newsletters' trading practices. Here's why: serious refunders (and couponers) keep very organized files, containing store receipts and proofs-of-purchase from every product they buy. Most offers are limited to one per household. But it's very possible that one person will have on hand some surplus offers he or she can't use. Through newsletter ads, refunders can sell or trade these "complete deals" or forms.

Unfortunately, the manufacturers of coupon and refund forms take a dim view of trading. According to *The Tightwad Gazette,* in 1994, newsletter publisher Ellen Biles of Georgia received 21 months in prison on four counts of mail fraud: Ellen submitted multiple refunds for the same offer and sold "complete deals" through the mail to an undercover postal inspector.[7] Amy Dacyczyn advises refunders to play it safe, submitting refunds only for products you bought, sending in exact purchase receipts, and reading the fine print carefully. Mary Kenyon agrees, adding that it's important to use only one address, one offer per family (if specified on the form), and legitimate cash register receipts for refund requests.

With all this in mind, refunding can be an enjoyable hobby that saves some money on food. You'll find refund forms in the same places as coupons, and also on bulletin boards in stores, at courtesy desks, on specially marked packages, and even at cashiers' counters.

To learn more about refunding, refer to the publications listed in Resources.

So there you have it, several ways to beat the system at the store. And did you know there are other strategies you can use to cut your grocery bill, even without setting foot in a supermarket? Chapter Three shows you how.

NOTES:

1. This tip comes from *The Tightwad Gazette* newsletter.

2. Price Club has now merged with Costco to form PriceCostco. See listing of warehouse clubs in Appendix Two.

3. *The Frugal Times* newsletter is currently out of print. Back issues are owned by *The Penny Pincher,* and this excerpt is used with permission. See Resources.

4. From *Saving Money Any Way You Can,* page 59, ©1994 by Mike Yorkey. Published by Servant Publications, Box 8617, Ann Arbor, MI 48107. Used with permission. See Resources.

5. From THE SHOPPER'S REPORT by Barbara Salsbury. Used with permission. See Resources (Miscellaneous Products and Videos).

6. From *Saving Money Any Way You Can,* pages 43–44, ©1994 by Mike Yorkey. Published by Servant Publications, Box 8617, Ann Arbor, MI 48107. Used with permission. See Resources.

7. From *The Tightwad Gazette* newsletter, February 1994 and April 1994.

CHAPTER 3

Other Ways to Beat the System

One of the frustrating aspects of writing this book is that just when I think I've covered it all, new information comes in. Consider these ways to save on food: belonging to a co-op, bartering, organizing better for better savings, meal planning, cooking once a month, mega-cooking®, making or cooking more of your own food, gardening, preserving your food, gleaning, using government programs (as a last resort), and eating sensibly. What a list of strategies! If you don't enjoy shopping at grocery stores—or can't save as much as you'd like to there—then several other cost-cutting options are available to you.

BELONG TO A COOPERATIVE

When I began to seriously investigate cooperatives, I discovered the National Cooperative Business Association. They offer a free listing of helpful publications you can buy to learn more about co-ops. I called NCBA and requested their no-cost, how-to-get-started packet and found it very informative.

What advantages are there in joining a food buying co-op? Members are attracted for a number of reasons, some as simple as socializing with like-minded neighbors, some as noble as helping our environment by eliminating much of the packaging used in supermarket foods.

Another important drawing point is big savings—at least over health food store prices—on organic foods. I consulted a catalog from Blooming Prairie Warehouse in Iowa City, Iowa, supplier for nearly a dozen co-ops in the St. Louis area. Selection is large and varied. Local co-op contact person Laurie Lowe explained, "Many members are concerned not only with cost, but also in buying quality organic and natural products." Laurie particularly likes the delicious cheese she purchases through Blooming Prairie.

Just how does a co-op operate? Jane Dewey, sales manager at Northeast Cooperative, says they're "community groups that pool their resources to buy groceries and produce in wholesale quantities at wholesale prices. Participating in a preorder co-op involves ordering food in advance of the delivery, consolidating household orders into a group order, placing the order with a wholesaler, unloading it from the delivery truck, breaking it down into household orders, collecting payment and keeping accounting records."[1]

Most wholesalers do require a minimum order of at least $500, but several families buying together can add up dollars quickly. The more you order, the more you save, so to speak.

A majority of co-op members are involved with one of the huge warehouses, like Blooming Prairie. But options vary widely. Jill Bond, author of *Dinner's in the Freezer,* says individuals may be able to work with wholesalers directly: in other words, if you preprepare food in large quantities and place one $500 order once a year, you don't need to "cooperate" with anybody else. And of course, you can organize a very informal—or very small—co-op. Not long ago, I met a woman whose circle of friends took turns buying produce from Produce Row, a kind of farmers' market for wholesalers, here in St. Louis. Every week, one of the four families collected everyone's money and bought ultrafresh fruits and vegetables in quantity, at wholesale prices, then delivered one-fourth of the goods to each family.

There are advantages to these smaller, informal co-ops, such as more flexibility and greater control over getting exactly what you want. But connecting with a warehouse does offer tremendous choice. Blooming Prairie's 150-page, fine-print catalog goes into great detail: it even tells you if any given food is fruit juice-sweetened, has salt, wheat, or yeast in it, and meets organic standards. Members are also assured that they will receive plenty of help, including access to technical and computer support, a lending library, meetings and seminars, a newsletter, and more.

Joining any kind of food buying co-op requires involvement. Depending on the organization, you may be asked to help recruit members, plan meetings, order, do paperwork, bag, divide into individual orders, and more. Some storefront co-ops request their members wait on customers in the store. And others will allow you to forego all the work if you're willing to pay more.

Finding the time to help may be a problem. Because many families these days have very few spare hours, the Michigan Federation had at one time "introduced a new type of buying club, in which a coordinator is paid 9 percent of the sales of the club for doing all of the work," says Joel David Welty, author of several publications on co-ops. "For some clubs, this can mean extra income of $450 a month for the coordinator."[2] You organize and run the co-op, you get the price breaks, *and* a commission. This may be an option for some.

As with any kind of food buying, self-restraint is a must. Take convenience foods, for example: co-ops offer them, just as the supermarket does. In one of Blooming Prairie's catalogs, I found items as diverse as "Raviolini with Vermont Cheddar and Walnuts," "Jumbo Oat Bran Fruit Bars," and "Jammin' Corn and Potato Chowder." Whatever its form, recipe, or brand name, a convenience food is still more expensive than making it yourself. Those who buy through a co-op must be just as shrewd in their purchases as those who buy at stores.

Does belonging to a co-op really save you money? That depends. Is it important to you to purchase organic raisins? Are you allergic to milk, and presently buying soy substitutes at a health food store? Do you use only olive oil—rather than generic vegetable oil—in your cooking? Then a co-op may be a cost-saving option.

On the other hand, if your eating habits are more meat-potatoes-and-apple-pie (hopefully the *healthier* versions), you'll need to take a close look at what co-ops sell and how that relates to what you buy. Compare prices carefully; you may be able to acquire quality, healthy food more cheaply at local stores and outlets. Also remember that some, though not all, local organizations charge membership fees. Once informed, you'll be able to make an intelligent decision about whether or not cooperatives might save you money on your weekly grocery bill.

I have to admit that researching co-ops has made me reconsider joining one myself. Blooming Prairie's catalog contains especially good prices on some items I regularly use, like yeast and spices. They also offer "deep discount deals" each month. Buying in case stack volume may yield discounts ranging from 10 to 30 percent. You can even order a sample package of several foods (usually new industry products) to try for a low price. And then there's that good cheese I keep hearing about. . . .

If you're interested, refer to Resources (U.S. Cooperative Food Warehouses) to locate a co-op in your area. Maybe I'll see you at the next meeting.

BARTER

Years ago, when I taught piano lessons, I bartered a semester's worth of lessons for several pounds of prime Wisconsin cheese. My student's father owned a cheese factory, so it was a real bargain for her and a lot of delicious free food for me.

One-on-one bartering is not uncommon. But now there's a new, more complicated twist: trade networks that help businesses to work with each other on a noncash basis. Although rules vary among these networks, the principle is basically the same: several businesses band together in a trade exchange, which lists their services or products to other members. When Company A "sells" $1,000 worth of services to Company B, then Company A receives $1,000 worth of trade dollars. Those trade dollars, in turn, can be used to "buy" goods or services from other businesses in the exchange.

N.C.E.

Our neighbors, specialists in chimney repair, told me about National Commercial Exchange. The Bufords had just joined N.C.E. Already they had cashed in some trade credits earned through their work for $700 worth of pediatric dental work, plus eyeglasses valued at $223. Because they are members of an exchange, the Bufords did not have to trade dollar for dollar with one individual. They could have bartered their earned trade credits with a restaurant, caterer, or even a cheesecake company. (I'll bet you were wondering how I was going to relate all this to food.)

I called N.C.E. and learned that the local chapter is part of a national network. The St. Louis Association currently lists no supermarkets, but had at one time included some. N.C.E. or other bartering exchanges in your area may offer that option. By joining, you might be able to trade some of your personal goods and services for fruit baskets, wedding cakes, a catered dinner party, an evening out at a fine restaurant, or just plain groceries.

When a business joins National Commercial Exchange, it is billed a one-time membership fee of $500, half of which can be paid in barter. In addition, the purchaser pays a 10 percent cash commission to the office each time a product or service is received. Sellers call N.C.E. for an authorization number and the buyer's account is credited. Receipts are kept by all parties, including the office. Members receive a detailed monthly statement recapping all purchases. There are also renewal fees yearly; each exchange has a different format.

In addition to record-keeping, exchange organizations actively promote participating businesses in a number of ways. N.C.E. in St. Louis mails a monthly newsletter that includes advertising and lists of what members want. If a needed service or business is not already part of N.C.E., the association tries to enlist one.

Share

Joining a trade organization may or may not qualify as an important means of saving money on food. But there is another option. Meet SHARE, Self Help and Resource Exchange, headquartered in San Diego, California. SHARE is a nonprofit, national program whose primary goal is "to build community by helping people work together to stretch their food budget."

Here's how it works. A community organization—a church, tenants' group or club, for example—fills out an application to become a host organization. This host provides a place where members and people in the neighborhood can register for discounted food packages. Each package is the same within each region, a $25 to $30 value for $14. The standard version always includes six to 10 pounds of meat, four to seven fresh vegetables, two to four fresh fruits, pasta, rice, or cereal, and a few specialty items. Both vegetarian and mini-packages (half the usual amount and price, ideal for seniors and small families) are also available in some areas.

At registration, participants pledge two hours of community service for every package to be purchased. Pledges can be fulfilled through normal church and volunteer activities, or even through helping to package bulk foods at the SHARE warehouse. The host organization tallies the number of packages requested, places an order with local SHARE headquarters, and sends a team of volunteers to pick up and bring back the food.

SHARE doesn't quite fit into a "bartering" or "cooperative" category. The program is open to everyone who is committed to consistent community participation, so in a sense, a discounted food package is bartered for volunteer work. SHARE's volume-buying power gives it some of the advantages of—though little similarity to—a cooperative.

SHARE is rapidly expanding and may be in your area now or in the near future. To find a nearby location, see Resources.

GET ORGANIZED

Have you ever stood in your kitchen at 4:45 P.M., dismally scanning the shelves for ideas for dinner? That's me sometimes, hoping for miracle food that assembles itself fast and easily on the table. It doesn't happen! No need to panic; there *are* alternatives to chaos.

Meal Plan

We all know how to meal plan, right? We take out a calendar, jot down dinner menus for each day of the month, and we're all set to have picture-perfect suppers. At least that's the idea, and basically, it's a good one. By planning ahead, we usually assure our families of better-quality, good-tasting, healthy food and adequate nutrition.

If you're looking for inspirational meal plans, I suggest a browse through your library's cookbook section; almost every cookbook has dozens of helpful ideas. When designing the menus, here are some general principles to keep in mind.

1) Make sure to allow space for leftovers. If you've already "booked" every day for October, and nobody's having last night's soup for lunch, you might want to leave a night free now and then for all the odds-and-ends eating.

2) Don't feel guilty if you fail to have gourmet dinners on the table every day. We sometimes have better things to do with our time than cook.

3) Plan variety, but also keep in mind what your family likes. I recently read a cookbook that said something like, "There's no excuse for fixing the same meal more than once every six months." That may be true for the adventuresome, but I don't think I could sell the idea to my children. If they had their way, we'd have pizza 365 days a year.

4) Be flexible. Meal planning can be expensive if you follow it

rigidly, passing up discounted and cheaper foods at the supermarket for the sake of "staying with the program." If fryers are on sale for 39 cents a pound, forget the round steak dinner this Wednesday and serve oven-baked chicken instead.

Do Once-a-Month Cooking

If you're really serious about meal planning, Mimi Wilson and Mary Beth Lagerborg may have the answer. These women have written a comprehensive book called *Once-a-Month Cooking (A Time-Saving, Budget-Stretching Plan to Prepare Delicious Meals)*. Mimi and Mary Beth not only cook all at once, they also do the majority of their monthly grocery shopping on one day.

They explain, "Each entree is partially prepared or cooked and assembled in advance. Then they're put into sealed containers and stored in the freezer. When you're ready to serve a certain meal, all you have to do is thaw it, combine the ingredients, and cook the entree. And all that time-consuming preparation and cleanup is done at one time."[3]

To help poor struggling cooks like me, Mimi and Mary Beth provide detailed shopping lists and menu plans. By using their system, they promise several benefits: ". . . after we've prepared a month or two weeks of meals, we don't have to fall back on less-nutritious, quick-fix foods or the more costly restaurant meals. . . . You can also save more money—and lots of time—when you make fewer trips to the store. Once you have your entrees in the freezer, you've done a major portion of your food preparation for the month."[4] If you're cooking once every 30 days using Mimi and Mary Beth's system, you will have 30 different meals prepared and in the freezer by the end of one long cooking day.

The major disadvantage I can see to once-a-month cooking is this: when one is shopping for ingredients for very specific meals, it is much more difficult to utilize store sales and other bargains. I think I come out ahead by serving flexible menus that make good use of specials. Still, the system seems worth considering, especially if it's adapted to accommodate cheaper, healthy foods. Many busy women I know swear by it.

Mega-Cook®

If you're really, *really* serious about meal planning, take once-a-month cooking a step further, to mega-cooking®. Jill Bond, author of

Dinner's in the Freezer, prepares *six months'* worth of entrees at one time. Jill, her husband Alan, and some of their four children work together as they cook huge batches of chili, lentil soup, sweet and sour meatballs, and 30 to 40 other kinds of dishes, all divided into dinner-size servings and frozen for later use. This system differs from once-a-month cooking in that many batches of *the same dish* are all prepared at one time.

Jill's system of mega-cooking® encourages the use of the reader's favorite recipes. You can cook as expensively—or economically—as you like. There's also a tremendous cash advantage to buying in such large quantities. A mega-shopper® can purchase the biggest (and cheapest) sizes of canned goods, crates of fresh, low-cost produce from the farmers' market, and discounted meat from a butcher who sells 20-pound packages at near-wholesale prices. From a survey the Bonds conducted of people using their program, they found families averaging a yearly savings of $1,640 over what they were spending on groceries the year before.

How does mega-cooking® work? The organization required is, as you'd expect, thorough. Jill's family usually devotes much of a weekend to preparing about 180 meals. To help others streamline their own system, *Dinner's in the Freezer* provides a myriad of blank forms—like "Tasks to be Done" and "Sample Timing Chart"—as well as plenty of good advice. Jill also offers workshops nationwide to help would-be mega-cooks® get started.

I know what you're thinking: who in the world would want to spend so much time preparing so much food? *Dinner's in the Freezer* assures us that cooks actually save dozens, perhaps hundreds, of hours in the long run. For example, if I average one hour a night doing cooking and cleanup for 180 dinner meals, I've invested 180 hours (although I still have to wash the plates and silverware, of course; the Bonds do, too!). Jill, Alan, and their children get the same job done in less than 20 hours, or about 50 hours of combined work. They save even more time by avoiding frequent trips to the supermarket. The result: a *lot* of free hours!

Mega-cooking® can start small, of course, as once-a-*week* cooking, or even something as simple as doubling tonight's lasagna recipe, then freezing the second portion. Some of us can't afford the cash outlay required for buying in big quantities, and some of us enjoy being in the kitchen and really don't relish the thought of having most of it done in advance. For others, though, mega-cooking® is appealing. Apart from saving both time and money, there's something to be said for having a freezer full of "preprepared" food on hand.

Use Leftovers

Menu-planning is one part of good organization. Another, equally important, is wise use of leftovers. Rule #1 is to keep a tight inventory, either mental or written, of foods on hand in the freezer, cupboard and refrigerator. Here are some ideas for using leftovers.

- Breads of all kinds: Freeze until you have a bag full. Make stuffing, garlic breadsticks, bread pudding, bread crumbs, or croutons.
- Fruits: use in Jell-O, popsicles, or Frozen Fruit Delight (see Recipes). Ripe bananas work well in banana bread or cookies.
- Leftover turkey: make soup, pot pie, or enchiladas.
- Vegetables: chop or puree and add to ground meat dishes, or store in a freezer "soup pot," ready to simmer when you have a pot's worth.
- A variety of leftovers: serve for lunches or snacks. Or make a buffet night where you serve dabs of this and that along with a special dessert.

Most of the above ideas are mine, and I must admit I've been pretty proud of my expertise in thinking of them. Then I discovered *The Use-It-Up Cookbook (A Guide for Minimizing Food Waste)* by Lois Carlson Willand. Now this is a truly comprehensive treatment of leftovers! Included are 190 pages of recipes and good advice, a reheating time chart, storage guide for perishable foods, detailed index, and much more. Name just about any food you can think of, and you can find it here, along with dozens of ways to creatively recycle it. See Resources.

Try the 24-Hour-in-Advance Meal Plan

Amy Dacyczyn, author of *The Tightwad Gazette* (both a newsletter and two books), suggests a system of organizing meals that involves minimum advance planning.

Amy and her husband, Jim, scout out the best deals on food, then inventory their home supplies before buying. Most of their shopping is a once-a-month outing. But they don't hesitate to make a special side trip, when running errands, to stores with particularly good deals. They also stock up on larger quantities of food that go on sale less often.

Actual meal planning occurs the night before, 24 hours in advance. Either Jim or Amy decide what to serve for dinner tomorrow, considering "what type of meal we haven't eaten in a while, what we have a surplus of, what the weather will be like (so we can make hot meals on cool days, and vice versa), what our schedule will be, who will be home, what garden vegetables are ripening, and so on."[5]

The Dacyczyns say this type of meal planning, 24 hours in advance, works very well for them. They can thaw frozen foods, soak dried beans, and prepare what's needed for slow cooker meals ahead of time. I think their system has merit, and have often used it myself. Here are two points to consider when trying this strategy.

1) Keep your menus varied. One week, while trying a let's-just-use-up-what's-on-hand, last-minute strategy, I ended up preparing the same foods over and over again, to the point where even my children were bored (and *that* takes some doing). We had three consecutive meals based around some kind of meat and low-fat gravy recipe. I would guess Jim and Amy avoid this scenario, as they think about what they *haven't* eaten in a while. But I do think it's easy to get lazy with this strategy.

2) Although I don't like rigid meal plans (and neither do the Dacyczyns), there's no reason why you can't draw up some kind of flexible plan. Most people operate better with an outline. Better to be too structured, then relax, than to be too relaxed, then try to structure. In other words, I'd rather have the makings of some great meals on hand and not use them, than have most (not all) of what I need and try to make the best of it.

Do 15-Minute Cooking

A friend of mine recently said to me, "I can't spend as little on groceries as your family does because I just don't have as much time to cook as you do." Her remark was such a surprise to me that, for a moment, I'm afraid I just stared at her stupidly. You see, I have a well-kept secret, one that's revealed in my book, *15-Minute Cooking* (see Resources): I spend *very* little time in the kitchen each day.

Instead, I've developed a system I call "15-minute cooking," one that started years ago when I had a house full of active little ones and no time for much of anything besides the children. Eric was born the day before my 33rd birthday, and overnight my life changed from one of almost total freedom, to being on call 24 hours a day, trying to pacify a very demanding infant. Then came Christian, 19 months later. By the time Eric turned four, Christian was a wild-man toddler and I also had a baby, Lisa. That was a circus, I can tell you! (Many of you know what I mean.) Michael was working most evenings, so in order to get any kind of a dinner on the table, I found I had to prepare food in very short segments. There was *never* an extra hour or two available for uninterrupted cooking.

Now, out of years of habit, I still plan most of my recipes and menus so that food can be prepared in two 15-minute sessions a day, one session sometime in the morning, and another right before dinner. Obviously, there are many foods you *can't* cook using this system. You can't make a yeast bread that has to be kneaded and left to rise several times during the day. You can't make complicated entrees, or really fancy desserts. Baking time is not included in this system; what we're talking about here is hands-on preparation only. But it's surprising what you *can* prepare in just two 15-minute sessions: home-cooked entrees, side dishes, hot breads, and desserts. With such short time periods required, I've found it much more manageable to assemble a first-rate meal.

Almost every food in this book's Recipes section, with the exception of the yeast breads, can be adapted to 15-minute cooking. You might start the vegetable beef soup in the Crock-Pot® first thing in the morning, for example, and right before dinner, make popovers, dice carrot coins, steam broccoli, and prepare a quick gelatin dessert for tomorrow night. Next morning, prepare salmon croquettes and mix up corn bread. Store these in your refrigerator until evening, when you can oven-bake both the salmon and cornbread, and also open a can of peaches and assemble a cauliflower/broccoli salad.

The system takes practice, until you get used to overlapping easier-to-prepare dishes with harder ones. You also have to have quick recipes on hand. But as you can imagine, 15-minute cooking is not only healthy, with an emphasis on fresh, nutritious foods, but also a real time-saver. I think we're all more enthusiastic about cooking— especially on the really hectic days—when we know it's going to be *fast*. That knowledge helps to motivate us to stay home rather than eating out, saving money, too. The 15-minute cooking system works very well for our family. Perhaps it would work well for yours, too.

In summary, organization in meal planning can really run the gamut: plan six months' in advance, plan 24 hours in advance, use up your leftovers creatively as you cook, try 15-minute cooking, and/or wing it completely. What's best? That's up to you to decide!

MAKE OR COOK YOUR OWN

In Chapter Two, I listed several ways to save money when buying specific, healthy foods at the store. Another alternative is to save money when *preparing* these same foods. Then, if you buy an item cheaply and also cut some of the preparation costs, your savings are doubled. (Starred areas are featured in Recipes.)

Meats and Other Proteins

Let's say, for example, that you've just bought a whole chicken for 39 cents a pound. To save even more in cooking, you can dish up small helpings, or stretch a few ounces a long way in a casserole, ethnic dish, or hearty soup.

Perhaps you can substitute more vegetarian dishes in your diet and make even better use of your food dollars. A variety of healthy foods (from USDA's food pyramid or the basic four food groups) will add up to what you need in the course of a day, even without meat. Jackie Iglehart, editor of *The Penny Pincher,* prepares several dishes from cooked beans; she buys 25-pound bags of dry pintos from a food co-op for 41 cents a pound. By teaming beans, homemade breads, grains like brown rice, several vegetables and fruits, the Igleharts are able to serve low-cost, protein-rich meals for 25 to 50 cents per person.

Don't purchase boneless, skinless chicken breasts at premium prices when you can buy a couple of whole chickens and "make your own" breasts: debone them yourselves, and remove the skin. If *I* can do this, *anyone* can, and it only takes five minutes. You'll have several more pounds of meat left over for the same price you would have paid for two measly breast portions.

Cheaper meat tastes better when prepared carefully. Marinades and tenderizers improve both quality and texture, and they need not be expensive. Mary Ellen, in *Mary Ellen's Helpful Hints,* suggests rubbing a roast with a marinade of vinegar and oil, then letting it stand in the refrigerator for two hours before baking. Or slice meat very thinly with a sharp knife, then marinate. Jill Bond sometimes uses orange or pineapple juice.

I often cook meat with a Crock-Pot®; eight hours yields fall-off-the-bone texture, and every tidbit is used. Pressure cookers are another option, especially when preparing tougher meats. Some cuts, like beef brisket, can be covered with water in a Dutch oven, simmered for three or four hours until tender, and sliced thinly across the grain.

Dairy Foods

Before you shop the dairy aisle, be aware that there are a number of substitutions you can make at home to save money. Dry milk is often—not always—less costly than liquid, especially if you follow directions carefully and don't load up your drink or recipe with extra powder. Use dry milk powder to make your own sweetened condensed milk* and sugar-free, low-fat cocoa*. Create homemade, low-fat sour cream* in the blender. Another dairy substitute, one for whipped topping*, can also be created from scratch. Homemade sherbert* is incredibly easy, nutritious, and cheap.

If you use margarine, you can save considerably by purchasing stick rather than tub versions. And did you know you can make your own inexpensive soft "diet" margarine, one that is lower in fat than the regular version? Using a beater, thoroughly blend skim milk into a pound of margarine. You'll have to experiment to see what works best for you, but I've found that I can add almost a cup of skim milk per four sticks. If you prefer butter, substitute stick butter and add milk to that.

You can also create your own yogurt*. Several years ago a neighbor shared with us several large boxes of nonfat milk powder; she received them free and never used them. When I picked up a yogurt maker for $1 at a garage sale, we began churning out yogurt for nothing! The process is very easy, with or without a machine. And you'll save significantly: if milk is $2 a gallon, homemade plain yogurt costs about 12 cents a cup. Yogurt is good not only for snacking, but also as an inexpensive, healthy substitute for sour cream and mayonnaise.

Breads, Grains, Cereals

Save on breads, grains, and cereals by cooking a quick, nutritious breakfast. In her booklet, *The $30 a Week Grocery Budget,* Donna

McKenna lists the following mainstays for breakfast at her house: hot cereals, oatmeal, Cream of Wheat, French toast*, muffins*, pancakes*, and waffles. Jackie Iglehart, publisher of *The Penny Pincher,* makes open-faced sandwiches under the broiler, like her "melt-down," an English muffin topped with a thick tomato slice and thin piece of cheese. Cook hot breakfast cereals overnight in your Crock-Pot.® Any of these options is much cheaper than cold cereal with milk, and all can be prepared nutritiously.

Jackie also recommends using a breadmaker. She claims that, even with an initial outlay of $234, her machine paid for itself in a few months and now saves her $500 a year over store-bought bread prices. A baker sells flour and yeast at cost to Jackie, enabling her to produce a loaf of homemade bread for 15 cents. Amy Dacyczyn, author of *The Tightwad Gazette,* thinks breadmakers are overrated. If you'd like to read both sides of the debate (well worth it before you buy a breadmaker), plus additional information on kitchen appliances, see Appendix Three.

Another option is to keep a big batch of yeast bread dough in your refrigerator. *More-with-Less Cookbook* says any dough with at least one tablespoon of sugar per cup of flour can be stored chilled for up to three days. Spray the top of the kneaded dough with nonfat cooking spray, cover with plastic (first) and a damp cloth, then refrigerate. Punch down as needed. Bring dough to room temperature two hours before baking, and let it rise until doubled, about one and a half to two hours. Bake as usual.

To cut baking costs and eliminate most or all fat, follow the advice in *Secrets of Fat-Free Baking,* an informative recipe book by Sandra Woodruff. Woodruff says you can replace all the fat in cakes, muffins, quick breads, etc. with fruit purees, applesauce, and fruit juices; nonfat yogurt and buttermilk; honey, molasses, jam, corn syrup and chocolate syrup; prune butter and prune puree; and mashed pumpkin, squash and sweet potatoes. I've tried this with several recipes, and found the "secrets" really work. You won't believe how many loaves of bread I've made from last year's recycled Halloween pumpkin, and free pumpkin is more nutritious and cheaper than canola oil! (The only drawback is that, in some recipes, you have a *lot* of sugar. See Resources.)

Here are more fat-reducing—and sometimes money-saving—baking tips:

- Use two egg whites in place of every whole egg. We've found buying whole eggs, then discarding the yolks, is cheaper than buying the prepackaged, low-fat product.
- Add cocoa to recipes calling for chocolate. Three tablespoons plus a little sugar replaces one square of baking chocolate or ¼ cup chocolate pieces.
- Coat pans with nonstick cooking spray rather than buttering and flouring. (This is actually more expensive, but may be worth it in the long run when it comes to health benefits.)
- Cater to recipes that feature cheaper whole grains, such as oatmeal bread instead of whole wheat bread.
- Grind your own wheat into flour. See Appendix Three for more information.
- Leave out nuts if they are prohibitively expensive, or use a cheaper variety, like peanuts.
- Try to bake several items at once; I like to bake muffins at the same time I'm preparing a casserole, and save on energy costs.

Baby Food and Formula

Nurse if you possibly can, and for as long as you can. You can't beat the cost, convenience, or nutrition! La Leche League International will be glad to answer any questions you may have on breast-feeding, and there's no obligation or fee. See Resources.

When your infant is ready for more solid food, check the local library for books on making your own baby food. To tell you the truth, my children went from nursing full time to slightly bland, mashed-up table food. I sometimes pureed leftovers and froze them in ice cube trays, then microwaved what I needed at the last minute. Most of the time my babies ate right along with us. Of course, caution must be taken: no honey for children under a year old, for example, and no nuts. Hot dogs and grapes must be cut into minuscule pieces. Ask your pediatrician for guidelines.

Drinks

We make orange juice from frozen concentrate, as Aldi's brand is much cheaper than ready-made; compare prices in your area for the best buy. If my children have reached their daily quota of milk products, I serve them orange juice for dinner: it beats soda and Kool-Aid, which we used to have more often (I was still offering Kool-Aid when recording some of the menus in Chapter One and Appendix One).

We also drink ice water in the car when we're out and about, between meals, and as "seconds" at meals.

Jackie Iglehart (of *The Penny Pincher* newsletter) converted from spending over $200 a year on bottled seltzer to making her own for about $47 a year. Jackie bartered her graphic design skills for a $250 seltzer-maker from a National Safety Association (NSA) distributor.[6] What's a seltzer-maker? It's a plastic unit that contains a refillable CO_2 canister and a place to attach a one-liter bottle. The canister supplies enough "fizz" for at least 200 bottles, though the Igleharts say they get many more than that. When the CO_2 is depleted, you can have the canister refilled for $19 plus shipping. Meanwhile, your seltzer-maker "spritzes" water, a fruit juice/water mixture, or even flat soda, by adding CO_2. The Igleharts' machine paid for itself in a little more than a year, and now their homemade seltzer averages less than eight cents a liter.[7]

Here's an idea for stretching coffee from Larry Roth of *Living Cheap News:* he takes the used grinds from a Mr. Coffee-type coffee maker, lets them cool, refrigerates, then adds new coffee to the existing grounds. Larry uses three and a half spoons for the first pot, and, for each subsequent pot, adds two and a half spoons until the filter is full. After that, he throws it all out and starts over. Larry says he can't tell any difference in the taste. For a gourmet-flavored coffee, try adding a pinch of salt, a little vanilla, or some cinnamon.

Also see the Recipe Index under "Drinks" for more ideas.

Popsicles*

This is a standard snack for us, especially in the summertime. I picked up two Tupperware mold sets at yard sales, and made my money back in two weeks. Usually I freeze fruit juice. But other ambitious parents I know have tried gelatin, pudding, yogurt, Kool-Aid, and just about anything else on hand.

Salad Dressings

I've found homemade dressings* and croutons* team up to make a delicious, inexpensive salad.

Sauces and Soups

Again, make your own. *More-with-Less Cookbook* says a good basic white sauce*, found in nearly every recipe book, takes about five minutes. From the parent recipe you can create cheese sauce, gravy*, and a number of variations, none of them high in fat or calories.

Broth is another commodity that's cheap and simple: add a little extra water to the roast or chicken you're baking, collect the liquid when you're finished, and skim off the extra fat. If you refrigerate the broth, fat solidifies at the top and is easily removed. I freeze excess broth and always have a supply on hand. Use it in homemade gravies, or start a soup pot in the freezer; when there's enough liquid, vegetables, and meat, you're ready to simmer up a stew.

Seasonings

You may want to purchase spices at discount or drug stores, or in bulk from a co-op, warehouse, or health food store, where they are almost always cheaper. But do try the recipe for taco seasoning* in Recipes!

Syrup

Make your own, low-fat maple-flavored syrup* and save at least 75 percent over store cost. Or try my delicious pancakes*: they're so moist they taste just fine with a simple dusting of powdered sugar.

In summary, as you trim your family's grocery bill, be on the lookout for ways to cut costs through preparing food yourself. It's an easy way to compound your savings!

GARDEN

We planted our first real garden a few years ago, and the whole experience was a dismal one. While the neighbors' tomato plants yielded dozens of firm, delicious fruit, our scraggly vines produced about ten. And a woodchuck from the nearby woods ate half of them. Our beans were so badly chewed we didn't get a single pod. Obviously we have much to learn about gardening.

Extension Services

Thankfully, there is help for people like me. I called our land grant university's extension service (Cooperative Extension Service). Off-campus faculty, so I'm told, translate the teaching and research of the university into workable knowledge for people of the state. When I spoke with the horticulture specialist at the University of Missouri, I was impressed with the scope of the program.

He sent me a listing of sample publications, most of them free or costing 25 to 50 cents each, on topics as varied as a vegetable planting calendar, mulching, soil preparation, how to grow specific fruits and vegetables, making your own compost bins, and dozens more. Some of the pamphlets are very specific, such as *Home Production of Black Walnuts and Nut Meats.* In short, your nearby Cooperative Extension Service (CES) should have just about everything you need to know regarding gardening and related topics. If you are unsure how to find such a program, refer to Resources (Organizations and More, Extension Service).

Gardening Books and Publications

A trip to the library can supply you with plenty of reading material. Look for gardening magazines or classics, like *Crockett's Victory Gardens* (Little, Brown & Co.). *Square Foot Gardening* (Rodale Press) tells you how to make the most of your garden space and conserve water and labor at the same time. *Gardening By Mail* (Houghton Mifflin Co.) is a sourcebook that lists what's available to you through mail order.

Gardening centers and nurseries may also feature a rack of good books. *All About Vegetables,* an Ortho publication, was recommended to me by horticulturists at the Missouri Botanical Gardens. Very specific sources like this one, as well as organic gardening magazines, are likely to be found at home and garden centers. Salespeople are usually knowledgeable and truly willing to help, and you can take advantage of their expertise. And while you're at such a store, peek into the encyclopedic *Ortho Problem Solver,* with answers to—and illustrations of—2,000 garden problems; many home and garden centers share their copy as a service to customers.

Jackie Iglehart has published two excellent special reports, *Penny Pincher's Garden Harvest* and *Penny Pincher's Landscape Makeover.* I followed Jackie's advice in setting up an easy compost pile, and plan to also plant fruit trees in containers, as her family does. See Resources.

Garden Clubs and Associations

Perhaps you would enjoy a more cooperative effort in your gardening. If so, local garden clubs may be the answer. The National Council of State Garden Clubs has chapters in all 50 states and another in the District of Columbia, and their 264,000+ members work together on a number of different projects, vegetable gardening included. Study courses are offered to members. *The National Gardener* magazine, leadership training, flower shows, a scholarship fund, and environmental activism are only a few of the many benefits available. To locate a chapter near you, see Resources.

Another option is sharing a community garden space. Many cities nationwide are reclaiming vacant lots and planting vegetable gardens. Write to the American Community Gardening Association to learn about opportunities in your area (see Resources).

I think I've found an answer to my "critters in the garden" problem, and I remain a hopeful gardener. With these kinds of resources available, even *I* may be able to manage a productive little vegetable plot next year. The Barfields' next project is a windowsill herb garden. Wish me luck.

PRESERVE YOUR FOOD

Let's assume that you've had a great yield on your garden (better than mine, anyway), and you have bushels of food to process. Or you've been to the farmers' market and returned home with a couple of crates of tomatoes and apples. What's next?

There's no point in me lecturing at length on the fine points of canning, freezing, and otherwise preserving foods, since I have little first-hand experience. So let me put you in touch with advice from some *real* experts.

First, at the risk of being repetitive, contact your local Cooperative Extension Service when you're ready to put away food. The University of Illinois Cooperative Extension Service sent me an inch-thick packet of canning and freezing fact sheets covering every topic imaginable: "Freezer Storage Chart," "Reduced and Sugar-Free Jams, Jellies and Preserves," and "Using Home-Preserved Foods Safely" are just a few of the varied titles. You can also find very specific information on processing particular foods, from tomatillos to paw paws to beef jerky (and more common foods, too, of course). Again, most of this information is free or near-free, and very much up-to-date. Guidelines for canning tomatoes, for example, have changed in the last few years, and a CES in your area can tell you exactly how and why.

Freezing

Nearly every standard cookbook explains the basics of freezing foods. If you preprepare meals through once-a-month or mega-cooking® (and already have one of the handbooks on hand), consult *Once-a-Month Cooking* and/or *Dinner's in the Freezer* for ideas on safely freezing foods. Jill Bond, in *Dinner's in the Freezer,* devotes an entire chapter to "Storing It All Away." Here are some of her suggestions.

1) Freeze carefully. Jill uses zippered, heavy-duty freezer bags and plastic containers with tight seals. She also recommends foil, clear plastic wrap, and freezer wrap applied generously and overlapped.

2) Label your food, including date and contents.

3) Keep an inventory of foods in your freezer. This can be as simple as a mental list, or as thorough as a write-and-wipe board, where items are erased as they're taken out of the freezer.

4) Freeze most of your foods in meal-size portions. An exception to this is an item like blueberries, which can be frozen in one large container, then retrieved in the quantity needed.

Canning

Several years ago, under a friend's watchful eye, I canned a big batch of pears and homemade applesauce from fruit I'd gleaned. This was my first experience with canning, and I really enjoyed it. In spite of the hard work, sweat, and sore fingers from all that peeling, there was something very satisfying about the end product, dozens of jars of food in my cupboards.

Canning really isn't difficult or expensive, say Pat Edwards of *Cheap Eating* and Amy Dacyczyn of *The Tightwad Gazette.*[8] It *does* require caution, good equipment, and a willingness to look for the best buys. You'll need canning jars (often available at yard or estate sales) in perfect condition, and basics like a colander, ladle, and funnel. For safety's sake, buy new lids; purchase them at salvage stores, or watch for sales. Many prefer a pressure canner instead of a regular canner, as it makes the process much quicker and enjoyable. It's very possible that you can buy quality used or discounted equipment as well as sharing with friends, and considerably cut your investment costs.

Why can when you have freezer space available? You and your family may prefer the taste; Michael and I can't stand frozen green

beans. Amy Dacyczyn also prefers the immediacy of canned foods—
as opposed to searching in the bottom of the freezer—and likes to
have canning as an option if extra food's available and the freezer's
full. She also points out that canned goods make nice gifts; freezer
foods don't fare too well under the Christmas tree.

Since this topic has to be either brief or incredibly detailed (and I
don't think I'll get into pickling, drying, smoking, or salting foods *at
all*), I'll close with recommendations from my two experts for *more*
expert advice in the form of two books: *The Ball Blue Book: The
Guide to Home Canning and Freezing* and *Putting Food By*. See
Resources.

GLEAN

There is much free and low-cost food available, and often it's only a
matter of finding and gleaning it.

For example, my sister-in-law Joan once worked out a deal with a
local supermarket. The produce department boxed up damaged produce and called Joan, who picked it up for free. I have not been able
to locate a store in my area that will do this, but it may be worth your
while to call nearby produce managers and at least ask. A few years
ago, when Joan came for a visit, she brought along three crates of
cucumbers and a huge box of all sorts of fruits, including strawberries, as a gift. And she still had plenty left over for her own family.

Sometimes orchards or farmers will let you pick "seconds" for free
or little cost. A major vegetable company owns fields near my home-
town and, after harvest, allows anyone interested to glean leftover
potatoes or green beans. A family friend, Eunice Welker, used to pick
a year's worth of free beans and can 100 quarts or more each summer.
Eunice says she has salvaged vegetables from other fields as well,
even when on vacation. She checks at local grain elevators to learn
harvest days, or simply stops to ask a farmer's permission to glean.

Pass the word around your neighborhood that you'd be glad to
take—and give—surplus food. One friend and I occasionally trade
leftovers: her family tires of the big roast they cooked on Sunday, and
we trade their meat for a loaf of my homemade bread. When a
neighbor moved, leaving behind her refrigerator contents, another
friend gathered up the goods and divided them with me. Last summer
we shared extra vegetables from my sister-in-law with our neighbors.

Gleaning is contagious! And in this way it really is possible to obtain free groceries.

If you plan ahead, you may be able to stock up on inexpensive produce in the summertime. Farmers' markets abound in both big cities and rural areas. Go late in the selling day, and preferably on the last selling day of the week, for some spectacular buys. You may walk away with boxes full of fruits and vegetables for practically nothing; friends of mine have. Also check out orchards and pick-your-own places, where fruits and vegetables are routinely cheap and sometimes, late in the season, *very* cheap.

Keep your eyes open for salvageable food that's going to waste. I've always loved to run and walk, and used to make it a point to try different routes. One autumn day I noticed an apple tree laden with fruit, much of it on the ground on a nice suburban lawn. Several more pass-bys confirmed that no one was picking the apples. Later that week, I stopped and asked the owner: would he mind if I cleaned up his yard in exchange for apples? He was delighted.

My two little boys and I made numerous trips to that man's backyard. We collected so many apples that I made several batches of applesauce and gave some away as Christmas presents. I sold dozens of bags of fruit to fellow workers. And we had enough apples, stored in a cool closet and eating at least four a day, to last us into January.

Another autumn, I was able to locate a pear tree and glean pears from a busy owner (that was the one that supplied pears for canning). I have also harvested several pounds of free hickory nuts. The food is there for those who are looking for it.

BENEFIT FROM GOVERNMENT PROGRAMS

Your taxes help support a number of different food programs, and you may need to take advantage of some of them when times are exceptionally hard.

As of this writing, USDA's Food and Consumer Service (FCS) provides these services[9]: Food Stamp Program; Special Supplemental Nutrition Program for Women, Infants and Children (WIC); National School Lunch Program; School Breakfast Program; Summer Food Service Program; The Emergency Food Assistance Program (TEFAP); Child and Adult Care Food Program; The WIC Farmers Market Nutrition Program; Commodity Supplemental Food Program; Special Milk Program; Food Distribution Program on Indian Reservations and the

Trust Territories; Nutrition Program for the Elderly; and Commodity Distribution to Charitable Institutions and to Soup Kitchens and Food Banks.

Your first step should be a call to the U.S. Department of Agriculture's Food and Consumer Service to learn about what's currently available (programs may have changed considerably since this writing). You can find their local number in the blue pages of your phone book.

EAT SENSIBLY

That's what this book is all about: eating sensibly. But as we discussed in the introduction, there is a difference of opinion as to what that means. My family and I are trying to take a healthy middle ground, one of cutting back on fat, sugar, and fatty meats, yet increasing our intake of fruits and vegetables, fiber, and whole foods.

We've found our food bills have gone down in some areas, as we buy much less meat, especially more expensive beef cuts, and practically no convenience foods. On the other hand, our produce bill alone averages between $10 and $13 a week. It takes a *lot* of fruits and vegetables to feed six of us "five a day," as the American Cancer Society recommends. Still, all of this is an investment in good health. I have seen a reduction this year in the number of colds and sick days we've all experienced, and I believe it's directly related to our new way of eating. Also, as some wise person put it, spending a few dollars a week on healthy food is a lot cheaper than bypass surgery.

Michael and I think of our new shopping and cooking strategies as a lifestyle change rather than a diet. But for those of you who are officially dieting, here's advice given by Melodie and Ron Moore in their newsletter, *Skinflint News* "Lose Pounds Not $:"

- Make your own diet meals by saving a variety of healthy leftovers in containers in the freezer, then reheating.
- Cook extra meat and slice thinly for a delicious diet lunch. Not only is the flavor much better, but you will also avoid the high-fat content of most packaged lunch meats.
- If you're craving sweets, have a small portion of a homemade brownie instead of buying those expensive "diet" frozen brownies.
- Eat plenty of fresh, seasonal fruit and vegetables.

- Take low-calorie snacks to work with you rather than facing the temptation of the vending machine.
- Drink lots of water or iced tea. For those who crave diet sodas, buy cans by the case.
- Exercise to cut your appetite.
- Consider forming or joining a support group rather than a costly weight-loss clinic.

Think of your dieting as a long term health benefit rather than a short term deprivation. You will be avoiding high-cost health problems brought on by extra weight.[10]

Are you amazed, as I was, to learn of so many ways to save money on groceries? Use some or all of these strategies—wherever you live, whatever your circumstances—and you really *can* eat healthy for $50 a week.

Just how does a family go about implementing these positive changes? The next chapter explains.

NOTES:

1. Reprinted from *NCBA Cooperative Business Journal.*
2. Reprinted from *NCBA Cooperative Business Journal.*
3 and 4. From "Once-A-Month Cooking," an article by Mimi Wilson and Mary Beth Lagerborg in *Focus on the Family Magazine,* April 1992.
5. From *The Tightwad Gazette,* issue #41, October 1993.
6. The Igleharts ordered their seltzer-maker from Kathy Martin, a National Safety Association (NSA) distributor in New York who sells all sorts of water and air treatment systems. If you cannot locate a local NSA distributor, call Kathy at 516-757-5088.
7. To read an entire article on seltzer-makers, order issue #6 (November/December 1992) from *The Penny Pincher* for $2. See Resources.
8. From *The Tightwad Gazette,* issue #56, January 1995 and Pat Edwards's book, *Cheap Eating.*
9. From *Nutrition Program Facts,* USDA, October 1994.
10. From "Lose Pounds Not $," an article in *Skinflint News,* January 1993.

CHAPTER 4

How Do I Ever Manage To Do All This?

Now that you've read several chapters, are you inspired enough to begin cutting back on your grocery bills? Or are you discouraged? Does it all seem too complicated and time-consuming?

Not long ago I attended a meeting where the speaker was supposed to motivate the rest of us to get organized. Unfortunately, just the opposite resulted. We all looked around rather hopelessly at one another, wondering how in the world we could *ever* accomplish what this woman did in a single day.

I hope you don't feel the same way about saving money on food. It does take time and organization, especially at first. But I guarantee that you can do it, once you find your own system, and save substantially in a relatively painless way.

But in order to demonstrate this a little more clearly, let me paint a hypothetical picture for you. Penny Price will be my make-believe person, the main shopper and meal planner for the Price family. Her husband John and three school-age children—Susan, Steve, and Danny—are also involved. Let's say that Penny has read this book and decides it's time to take action. We'll follow her and her family through a year and observe the changes in their lifestyle.

January 2: Penny shops as usual at her preferred store. She carries along a small notebook and jots down prices on stock-up items like cornmeal, skim milk, and whole grain bread. Penny takes a little longer than usual to check out store and generic brands and also writes down their cost in her notebook.

January 9:   This week, Penny stops by a nearby grocery store, one she seldom frequents simply out of habit. As she records prices in her notebook, she's surprised to find some items significantly cheaper than those at her usual store. She also discovers an out-of-the-way bin where marked-down meat is stored. Penny learns from the meat manager that surplus cuts are placed in the bin each morning, often at a 50 percent savings. While there, she stocks up on ketchup and oats, on sale at an exceptionally good price.

January 16:   Penny visits a large warehouse store with her price book. Cost-per-ounce signs help her decide whether buying in bulk would really save money. She concludes that some purchases, like dry cereal, low-fat cheese, and orange juice, are definitely cheaper at the warehouse, and she resolves to shop there once a month.

January 23:   At the breakfast table the morning before shopping, Penny compares two grocery store fliers and notes several items she needs on sale at National. She checks her price book and sees that the "loss-leader" foods are a good buy, cheaper than any other prices in the area. She does all her shopping at National this week.

January 30:   Penny checks out a meat market just across from the mall, right on her way home from other errands. She speaks with the butcher and gets some good advice on bargain cuts of meat and how to cook them. Penny buys chicken leg quarters on sale, several pounds at a considerable savings. She asks the butcher to wrap the poultry in two-pound packages and freezes all but one package for future use.

February 6:   Susan, eager to be a "good helper" to her mother, clips several coupons from the Sunday paper and arranges them in an envelope alphabetically. As Penny goes through supermarket fliers this week, she matches several sale items with coupons for even greater savings. She plans to shop at Schnucks, as they offer the best buys on what she needs, as well as double coupons.

February 13:   Penny takes a critical look at the kinds of goods she's been buying and decides to eliminate several convenience foods. This week, she purchases store brand tea bags rather than a six-pack of soda, bulk buy raisins instead of lunch-size packages, and generic toasted oats in place of name-brand cereal.

February 20:   John and the children sit down together and read through the book *Square Foot Gardening.* A visit to the library provides even more valuable information, including some gardening magazines and *Gardening by Mail,* a sourcebook on where to order supplies. Once they decide on the garden's layout, Danny and John plan to start seedlings in a warm, sunny corner of their walkout basement.

February 27:   The Prices have invited the Aldens for Saturday brunch, and plan a special "theme meal" with pancakes as the main dish. John prepares a huge batch of oatmeal pancakes the night before, first adding bananas, nuts, chocolate chips, and bits of low-fat cheese to four separate bowls of batter. When the Aldens arrive, a buffet is ready with syrup, honey, fruit sauce, yogurt, and ice milk as complements. The two families can't remember ever having so much fun at a company meal!

March 5:   Penny finds some intriguing new, low-fat recipes and decides to give them a try. First she whips up an easy nonfat French salad dressing. She makes her own croutons and bread pudding, using leftover whole wheat bread ends. She tries a basic white sauce recipe, adding mushrooms, to substitute for canned soup in the chicken casserole she's serving tonight. And she bakes a triple batch of applesauce gingerbread cake from scratch in less time than it takes to put together a single cake mix. Penny's hour in the kitchen saves the Price family about $15 . . . and several grams of fat per person!

March 12:   John decides to "brown bag" three times a week instead of eating lunch out. Susan, Steve, and Danny begin packing their own lunch boxes on the same days. John assembles barbequed chicken sandwiches, low-fat cheese slices, air-popped popcorn, carrot sticks with nonfat dip, raisins, pretzels, crackers, leftovers of all kinds, and homemade raspberry yogurt. The Prices estimate they can bank at least $20 weekly by bringing their own healthy food from home for noontime meals.

March 19:   John starts a new system for making coffee, a necessary expense in the Price household! He mixes grounds from the day before with new ones for a 50 percent savings. Penny cuts back to two cups of coffee a day and plans to drink more water instead.

March 26:   One brisk weekend day, Penny is in the mood for homemade bread. She tries a 90-minute recipe (see Cinnamon Yeast Bread in Recipes) and bakes four loaves. The children help, forming their own smaller dough balls, rolling them out, and sprinkling on cinnamon and sugar. Danny loves the taste of hot-out-of-the-oven bread so much that he asks to make it again soon. In a few weeks he is able to turn out loaves from start to finish all by himself.

April 2:   Penny visits the warehouse store again after an absence of several weeks. She is a smarter buyer this time around, and doesn't succumb, as she did during her first visit, to the temptations of boxed donuts and ready-made cheesecake. For breakfast the next morning Penny whips up a batch of healthy bran muffins. She makes a big batch of low-fat orange sherbert for dinner dessert. By *not* buying donuts and cheesecake—and substituting healthier, homemade sweets—Penny saves more than $8 on two items alone.

April 9:   Penny and John have made it a point to talk more frequently with Susan, Steve, and Danny about nutrition, and so have been both buying and eating healthier foods. When the children arrive home from school, they often fill up on celery with low-fat cream cheese, orange juice popsicles, or dry toasted oat cereal mixed with raisins. Fresh fruit has also become a favorite snack.

April 16:   Penny by now is quite a pro at using up leftovers, and the Prices waste very little food. Their freezer holds a large plastic container where leftover bits of cooked meat, vegetables, and broth accumulate until there is enough for a kettle of stew. Penny checks the refrigerator and shelves at least twice a week for odds and ends. Those foods that can't be recycled as soup are served at Thursday night dinner, smorgasbord-style.

April 23:   John goes shopping this week, checking out a new produce stand on his way home from work. The manager is anxious for business and talks with John for a few minutes about seasonal fruit and other bargains. Bananas are on special, six pounds for $1. John buys $10 worth of fruit, including several bunches of bananas.

April 30:   After a week of eating bananas twice a day, the Prices decide to freeze the excess. Some bananas are skewered on popsicle sticks and dipped in chocolate syrup, then wrapped in wax paper. The rest are pureed with a little lemon juice in a blender and frozen in two-cup containers, later to be used in banana bread.

May 7:   Penny and John sit down together and do some serious meal planning. They make a simple listing of 30 meals that nearly everyone in the family enjoys. Steve constructs a chart and helps arrange meals for the next month, projecting ahead for days the family will eat out and planning to be flexible as needed. In the meantime, Penny tries the 24-hour-in-advance plan, deciding on dinner meals the night before she prepares them.

May 14:   The neighbors down the street have joined a commercial exchange organization and tell the Prices about bartering. After careful consideration, John and Penny decide against joining. Instead, they contact several close friends and propose an informal kind of arrangement: any family who has a surplus will try to swap with another family who has a need. Penny agrees in advance to barter garden vegetables for the use of another family's pressure canner.

May 21:   The Prices make a joint decision to budget the amount of money spent in eating out together. After a couple of weeks of casually checking out restaurant coupons, they have decided that takeout pizza is their best bet. It's about half the cost of dining at their favorite steakhouse. They'll still splurge occasionally, of course. But by saving their restaurant money in a piggy bank, they'll soon have the extra cash they need to buy a family membership at the pool this summer.

May 28:   Penny and John have gradually made some major changes in their diet, and are thinner and more fit than they were six months ago. Everyone now eats less red meat and more beans, rice, and pasta; less sugary desserts and more nutritious alternatives. As they've cut their food bill, Penny and John have also cut their cholesterol levels and their weight.

June 4:　It's vegetable planting time! One warm Saturday the Prices bring seedlings up from the basement and ready the soil in their garden plot. They barter the use of a neighbor's tiller in exchange for John and Steve restacking the man's disorganized firewood. The Prices are also able to locate fertilizer and some needed tools on sale at a nearby nursery. The garden is planted by dinnertime.

June 11:　John, head gardener of the family, visits the University of Missouri's Cooperative Extension Service. He wants to get the latest information on "integrated pest management" so the Prices won't have to spend money on—and face health risks from—pesticides. John speaks in person with an expert advisor. He also takes home some free brochures on ways to maximize vegetable growth, build his own compost pile, and have the garden soil tested.

June 18:　John, Penny, and the children spend a Saturday morning at a pick-your-own strawberry patch. They've come at the end of the season and are able to glean berries at half the usual cost. The family picks enough to have plenty of homemade jam, strawberry desserts, and plain, delicious snacks.

June 25:　Sunday is a perfect summer day, and the Price family decides to spend the afternoon at the zoo. Their usual custom is to eat the food stand's overpriced hot dogs, popcorn, and soda. Today they pack a picnic instead. The $15 designated for a late lunch is used to purchase books at the zoo's gift shop.

July 2:　Three of the Prices have birthdays this month, and Penny decides to bake the cakes herself. She makes a triple batch of Very Best Fudge Brownies (see Recipes) and freezes three finished sheet cakes. Next comes a triple batch of frosting and again, two containers are frozen. Penny has already ordered *Baker's Easy Cut-Up Party Cakes* and the birthday boys and girl have decided on designs. Thanks to advance preparation, each cake requires less than 20 minutes for final assembly.

July 9:   The garden is growing nicely and the first crop of string beans comes in. The Prices cook a big batch for supper, using defatted ham broth for flavoring. As other produce ripens over the course of the summer, Penny contacts her friend about the swap they had agreed to earlier: use of a pressure canner in exchange for some vegetables. Now the family will be able to put up several quarts each of beans, peas, and tomatoes themselves.

July 16:   Penny learns that several church friends are organizing a co-op buying club. She attends an organizational meeting and carefully examines the supplier's catalog. For about an hour's worth of work each month, Penny can buy some products at a real savings, including bulk yeast, spices, low-fat cheese, and whole wheat flour. She joins the co-op.

July 23:   John, hungry for something home-baked, rescues pureed bananas and frozen strawberries from the freezer. A couple of hours later he's taking three large, steaming loaves of banana-berry bread from the oven. The Prices gobble down one loaf that night and enjoy generous slices for lunch the next two days.

July 30:   Penny's brother and his family are spending the weekend and the Prices intend to entertain them in style. Penny brings out lasagna and homemade French bread from the freezer, and makes a quick, five-minute chocolate custard pie for Friday night's meal. Saturday features a barbeque with grilled marinated chicken, corn on the cob, and fresh garden vegetables. Sunday dinner is turkey with all the trimmings. Penny's brother and sister-in-law enjoy the home-cooked meals, and are convinced their relatives have spent a fortune to feed them. (The Prices don't tell them otherwise!)

August 6:   Susan has become so skilled at using coupons that, shopping with her mother, she's able to save more than $7 at the store this week. Penny has promised that her daughter can bank any money saved on coupons, so Susan is especially attentive to good deals. She has even set up a coupon exchange box at the library and checks it regularly.

August 13:   John has just learned about a new farmers' market in the city, a 30-minute drive from home. Word has it that farmers there sell their goods at tremendous savings toward the end of the day. The Price family makes a trip downtown to check it out. They arrive late afternoon Saturday and, sure enough, come away with two large crates of fresh produce for a fraction of normal supermarket prices.

August 20:   Using some of the money they've saved on groceries, the Prices have purchased a used chest-type freezer. Penny has collected garage-sale containers all summer and has quite a stockpile. Vegetables and fruits from the farmers' market on Saturday are carefully sorted, processed, and frozen. Between the market's produce and their own garden's yield, the Price freezer is nearly full.

August 27:   A librarian approaches Susan as she checks her coupon trading box: has she heard about refunding? The librarian locates the name and address of *Refund Express*. Susan sends for a sample copy. She is amazed to receive an 80-page newsprint magazine filled with inspiring stories, numbers to call for free products, and hundreds of ads where swaps can be made for coupons and refund offers. Susan signs up as a subscriber.

September 3:   It's taken the Prices eight months, but their weekly grocery bill is now down to about $50. John and Penny's usual routine involves a trip to the warehouse store the first week of each month, where they stock up on lower-cost bulk items. The next three weeks Penny shops at one of two grocery stores, depending on which has the best specials and the best match-up with Susan's coupons. Penny also stops by the meat market occasionally. The produce stand, right on her way to one of the supermarkets, is usually so much cheaper that she often makes a quick run in for fruits and vegetables.

September 10:   Steve, riding his bike around the block, has noticed a neighbor's pear tree. Several trips by confirm that no one is picking the fruit. With Penny's approval, Steve leaves a note on the neighbor's door politely requesting that he be allowed to pick the pears. He gets a call the next day from an elderly man who's happy to have his fruit gleaned. Steve stops by one day after school and cleans the man's yard, carefully picking up the grounded pears that are salvageable. (The rotted ones are hauled home to the family compost pile.) Dozens are eaten for snacks. And the rest Steve sells door to door, collecting quite a sum for his "new bike" fund.

September 17: While out looking for garage sales, Penny notices an obscure day-old bread store and stops to investigate. The prices are excellent. She stocks up on whole grain bagels, dinner rolls, hamburger buns, and several loaves of oat bread. Penny freezes some breads and oven-toasts bagels. The rest are steamed over a kettle of hot water to almost-fresh quality.

September 24: The Prices have "put out the word" throughout their neighborhood that they will gladly accept any free food or goods, especially those that might otherwise go to waste. Soon friends are calling them: a hunter who has extra venison to share, a gardener who doesn't want to process all of her bumper tomato crop. The Prices graciously follow up with homemade bread loaves as thank-yous.

October 1: Autumn weather has everyone in the mood to pick apples. John, Penny, Susan, Steve, and Danny make a day of it at a nearby orchard, gathering over 50 pounds of fruit. They save about 70 percent compared to normal supermarket prices and have a wonderful time as well. The orchard owner supplies all three children with free small pumpkins as a bonus. Best of all, the whole family enjoys a wagon ride behind the farmer's tractor.

October 8: Penny has just read *Once-a-Month Cooking* and decides to try two weeks' worth of shopping plans and menus. She sets aside a Saturday morning for shopping and a Sunday afternoon and evening for cooking. The system works very well. Penny is surprised at how much is accomplished in a short time, and soon she has 14 entrees ready in the freezer. In a few months, she'll try mega-cooking®, then decide which system works best for the Price family.

October 15: Penny and the children decide to prepare for Halloween a little early this year. Together, they create an enormous batch of cookie dough and a triple recipe of caramel corn. Steve bags the caramel corn for his school party, and also helps Penny roll out dough and cookie-cut. Susan and Danny frost and decorate little pumpkin-shaped sugar cookies. The children don't mind their chores since the rewards—bites of treats—are definitely worth the bother.

October 22:   Susan wants to have a few friends over for dinner and a sleepover. The Prices agree, and set a $10 spending limit. No problem, Susan says. She scans her bulging coupon collection and pulls out several to use at a store offering double savings. She buys bread, deli meat packages, cheese, and soda on sale. With her coupons, they're only a fraction of the original cost. Susan also buys generic napkins and plates and glues on handmade autumn motifs. A menu for eight friends includes turkey and cheese sandwiches on buns, corn chips with homemade dip, carrot sticks, pretzels, caramel corn, cookies, and soda, all at a total cost of $9.68. (Hey, we can't eat perfectly healthy foods all the time!)

October 29:   John and the boys buy a large pumpkin from the produce stand and carve it for Halloween. The seeds are washed, dried, and oven-roasted. In a day or two the pumpkin itself will be cut into pieces, cooked and pureed in the food processor. Penny will make a few pies and have plenty left over to pop in the freezer.

November 5:   Halloween candy is on sale, so Penny purchases several large bags. She knows from experience that discounted candy bars and M&M's are often cheaper than baking chips. Penny freezes all the goodies in hidden reaches so no one will be overly tempted. Over the next few months she has a large cache of both treats and baking chocolate, for the children, of course!

November 12:   Thanksgiving is two weeks away and turkeys are on sale at the supermarket. Penny relies on her stockpile of other foods and spends most of the grocery budget on meat. She buys a whole turkey at 39 cents a pound and freezes it. She also invests in extra cranberries, reduced-fat margarine, whipped topping, and other sale items.

November 19:   Steve, the entrepreneur of the family, has found another source of income: nuts. While exploring a family friend's "back 40," he's located an out-of-the-way pecan tree. Steve gets permission to gather over a bushel and spends several hours shelling pecans. Penny and several neighbors buy large containers full of nuts for $5 each, still a good savings over store prices. Steve soon has another $35 to put in the bank. At this rate he'll have enough money for his new bike by spring.

November 26:   As the Prices celebrate Thanksgiving, they are truly thankful to God for their bountiful harvest of food. Penny has bought a second, fresh turkey and made her own low-fat stuffing and gravy. The menu also includes peas and potatoes from the garden. Using some of Steve's pecans, Susan and Danny have baked a banana nut loaf. John's special offering is his own cranberry relish, Penny's, a homemade pumpkin pie. The meal has been a real cooperative effort. But the results are outstanding in both savings and taste.

December 3:   Penny and a group of friends meet for an informal potluck at the Prices' house. The discussion turns to the astronomical cost of feeding a family, and Penny shares some of the strategies she's learned in the past year. Three women agree to try an informal swap of Christmas cookies next week in an effort to save both time and money. The Prices, the Aldens, and the Fergusons will each bake triple batches of three different recipes, delivering one batch of each to the others' homes.

December 10:   John is in the mood for Christmas shopping. Instead of heading for the mall, the family brainstorms some ideas for homemade presents. Danny wants to give his own special cinnamon yeast bread. Susan decides to make coupon holders, each with 50 coupons filed alphabetically inside. Steve plans to share jars of canned pears, the ones he foraged from a neighbor three months earlier. John and Penny will buy some items, of course. But for friends and coworkers, they decide to give assorted homemade muffins. They estimate a savings of at least $200 over last year, when most of their gifts averaged $25 per person.

December 17:   Penny has budgeted ahead, and plans to take advantage of holiday sales. The meat market has just advertised whole hams at half price, so she buys two. Susan is enthusiastically clipping coupons; many more are available now during the holiday season. Between both sales and double coupons, the Prices' grocery bill totals less than half of the regular cost of food.

December 24:   Penny and John exchange Christmas gifts shortly after the children are in bed for the night. Along with a few romantic offerings, John has also written out a coupon—good for five home-baked loaves of bread each week of the new year—for Penny (*and* the family). Penny can't decide which she likes better, her new perfume or that valuable coupon!

December 31:   As the new year rolls in, the Prices make a resolution: to save even more this year than last. They have learned much about ways to conserve the food dollar. Now they'll try their hand at other means of cutting back. Their goal is a family vacation to a ski lodge over the holidays next December. With the money they save, they'll be able to do it.

And so Penny, John, Susan, Steve, and Danny live happily ever after. And it *is* a fairy tale, I admit, and real life seldom runs so smoothly. The Prices cut healthy food costs in a very realistic way, one step at a time, one new strategy each week. That's what Michael and I have done, and it works. We actually practice much of what the Prices supposedly tried, and I know of many others who manage to accomplish this and much more. The composite picture is fictional but certainly possible.

The idea of my make-believe story is to inspire you. Wouldn't it be fun to write your own, *true* story this year?

CHAPTER 5

I Can't Save Money on Groceries Because . . .

The story of Penny Price is behind us now, and it's time to face reality! Do you think that, for you and your family, eating healthy for $50 a week is impossible? You spend a lot more than $50, but you have a good excuse, right? Then let's talk about it. Please fill in the blank below:

"I can't save money on groceries because _____."

Now allow me to anticipate some of your answers, and offer some suggestions.

"I can't save money on groceries because I'm too tired to cook and rely on convenience foods for most of my meals."

- Then do once-a-month or mega-cooking® on a weekend (or some other time when you're more rested) and make your own convenience foods.
- Try some of the recipes in the next chapter. Many entrees can be prepared in half an hour or less.
- Rely more heavily on time-saving devices—such as a Crock-Pot®, breadmaker, pressure cooker, or food processor—to make cooking faster.
- Menu plan carefully to allow for quick, easy, homemade meals on nights when you know you'll be most tired.
- Try *15-Minute Cooking,* my own system for cooking 15 minutes early in the morning (or right after dinner the night before), then

15 minutes just before dinner, for delicious, home-cooked meals. See Resources.

"I can't save money on groceries because I'm on a restricted diet and have to pay more for special foods."

For a low-fat and low-cholesterol diet:

- Calculate the number of grams of fat in the foods you eat, then devise an inexpensive diet with no more than 30 percent of total calories from fat. If, for example, you need 2,000 calories a day to maintain your weight, take 30 percent × 2,000 = 600 calories; 9 calories per gram of fat = 67 grams of total fat per day. Make healthy, cheap menu choices that keep your fat intake under 30 percent of your total daily calories (in this case, 67 grams).
- Combine double coupons with supermarket sales, and stock up on low-fat versions of margarine, sour cream, cheese, and other staples when they're cheapest.
- Do your own baking, but apply these fat and cholesterol-cutting rules: For cakes and soft-drop cookies, use no more than two tablespoons of fat per cup of flour. For muffins, quick breads, and biscuits, use no more than one to two tablespoons of fat per cup of flour (from *The New Lean Toward Health*). See other baking suggestions on pages 37 and 38.

For a diabetic diet:

- See the Recipes chapter for recipes reprinted from *Healthy Exchanges* newsletters. If you like what you try, I highly recommend your buying the *Healthy Exchanges* cookbooks, either directly from JoAnna Lund or in your local bookstore.

For healthier eating in general:

- Bulk-buy canola oil, brown rice, dry beans, and other healthy foods from a warehouse grocer or co-op.
- Think of meat as a side dish, and serve only small portions. Cook more chicken and turkey. Fortunately, both are usually cheaper than beef or pork.
- Learn to eat fish. Buy seafood that is currently in season. Better yet, take up fishing.

- Fill up on fresh fruits and vegetables, purchased in season from supermarket sales, produce stands, or farmers' markets.
- Serve beans. *More-with-Less Cookbook* features an entire chapter of bean recipes, some as simple as mashing cooked lentils, forming into patties and broiling like hamburgers.
- See Resources for highly recommended books on nutrition and healthy cooking. And of course, *read this book* cover to cover!

"I can't save money on groceries because I take my young children shopping with me, and I give in when they beg me for expensive treats."

- Then don't give in! (Easier said than done!)
- Talk to your children before you go to the store. Explain that you will be buying only what is on your list.
- Let each child choose one inexpensive treat per visit ahead of time. Any whining or obnoxious behavior forfeits the treat.
- Go to the store at a time when everyone's rested and fed.
- Involve the children in shopping, from fetching cans of corn to going through a pretend purse filled with "real stuff" (just like Mommy uses at the store).
- Take along special toys to keep little hands occupied and attitudes cheerful.
- Play quiet games or read a book during a long wait in the checkout lane.
- Combine firm rules with a pleasant experience, so resistance is minimized the next time.
- Reward well-behaved children with genuine praise. A favorite activity, extra privilege, or piece of candy doesn't hurt, either.

"I can't save money on groceries because I do a lot of entertaining."

- Then entertain with home-cooked meals whenever possible. Tablecloths, fresh flowers, candlelight, and delicious recipes make the simplest food seem elegant.
- Stick to cheap menus.
- Check out *More-with-Less Cookbook* from the library and read about Doris Janzen Longacre's "theme meals." Doris focuses on "one nutritious, cheap, but interesting dish," and adds a few

simple, complimentary dishes. Her suggestions are intriguing and inexpensive.

- Limit hors d'oeurves to cheaper varieties. Serve at tables rather than passing on trays.
- Host a potluck. You supply the main dish, dessert, drinks, and the house, and guests bring a vegetable, salad, and bread.
- Choose an "off-time" for entertaining. Offer only snacks or desserts.
- B.Y.O.B., wine coolers, soda, or juice.
- Read Melinda Tyler's booklet, *Party Panic: The Hesitant Homemaker's Guide to Planning the Perfect Dinner* for a wealth of ideas on home entertaining. Some of the suggested dinners are very inexpensive, and Melinda also tells you how to plan your own parties. See Resources.

"I can't save money on groceries because we're all big meat eaters, and meat is expensive."

- Then dine on cheaper cuts of meat, like chicken. Buy whole chickens and Crock-Pot® them (so meat falls off the bones easily) or cut into pieces yourself, using a sharp knife and a standard cookbook's directions.
- Buy a half or quarter side of beef from the butcher and divide it up, if necessary, with friends.
- Make it a point to only buy meat that's on sale. Stock up when your favorites are cheapest.
- Shop around for a supermarket that sells surplus, marked-down cuts. If your favorite supermarket doesn't have such a bin, ask the meat manager if he'd consider it.
- Gradually decrease the portions of meat served in your meals, and supplement with more breads, grains, fruits, and vegetables.

"I can't save money on groceries because my family drinks cases of soda—and other expensive drinks—every week."

- Soda usually goes on sale just before Memorial Day, the Fourth of July, and Labor Day. Stock up then, and hide all those extra cases in an obscure corner of the garage!
- Gradually substitute other drinks. We used to serve Kool-Aid to the children every night for dinner (it was cheaper than soda!).

Now we've converted to orange juice. Who says you have to serve juice for breakfast?

- If your family likes seltzer, consider investing in a seltzer-maker. Your machine "spritzes" water or a fruit juice/water mixture, enabling you to make your own seltzer for about eight to ten cents a liter, once the machine is paid for.
- See page 39 of this book for ideas on lower-cost coffee (and also information on ordering a seltzer-maker).
- See recipes for "homemade" drink ideas.
- Drink more water. If you can't stand the taste of tap water, try adding crushed ice and/or a slice of lemon. We have also found that water that stands in the refrigerator, open-topped, for a couple of days, tastes better. (I read somewhere that some of the chlorine gas in the water evaporates.)

"I can't save money on groceries because my children will only eat expensive, highly processed foods."

- Then introduce nutritious alternatives, one at a time, while gradually phasing out the junk. Find a healthy food, like grapes or bananas, that a child really likes, and serve it frequently.
- Begin to substitute raisins for candy, air-popped popcorn for potato chips, and homemade yogurt popsicles for ice cream bars.
- Remember that children go through phases. What they don't like today may become a favorite food tomorrow. Keep reintroducing *small* portions.
- We always put less on our children's plate than we think they will eat, though the servings are appropriate for their age and nutritional needs. Then, if Christian is hungry (which he nearly always is), he's welcome to have more. I've watched parents pile mountains of food on a child's plate, then constantly nag him to finish. In our minds, the less said about food—and the more said in pleasant dinner conversation—the better.
- Involve your children in cooking. When we checked out a "Superheroes" cookbook from the library, Eric could hardly wait to try—and eat—some nutritious recipes. See Resources, *DC Super Heroes Super Healthy Cookbook*.
- Serve food in a way that's attractive to children. Jill Bond, author of *Dinner's in the Freezer,* sometimes arranges her children's

salads in a sundae dish and calls her creation a "salad banana split." The banana is halved (as in a split) but filled with scoops of chicken or potato salad. Salad dressing, cottage cheese, and additional fruit complete this masterpiece. Jill says she's never had a child turn one down.

- Use "props" to make good food more appealing. Children who don't like milk may drink it from a special thermos or a "grown-up" glass with a special straw. Colorful plates and napkins help, too.
- Avoid food fights by giving children some choices. You can frame the question as "Would you rather eat your peas or banana bread first?" instead of threatening, "If you don't eat those peas right now you're in time-out for an hour!" (I've been foolish enough to say something like this last remark, and know how poorly it works!)
- Don't get into the habit of preparing whatever the child wants, especially if it's always different from the rest of the family's dinner. (There are exceptions to this, especially when you're dealing with a toddler on a temporary "food jag" who will only tolerate jelly sandwiches and applesauce.) Make a comment like, "I'm sorry you don't care for the chili, but this is what we're eating tonight. Would you like to help me prepare one of your favorite meals tomorrow night?"
- Offer no unhealthy alternatives. My children learned to drink water because, one summer, I simply told them that if they were thirsty between meals, they could have all the ice water they wanted. Now they help themselves to the pitcher in the refrigerator several times a day.
- Some parents tell me they insist their children finish what was left from the last meal before they eat anything else. In other words, if your child skipped his broccoli at dinner last night, he has to have broccoli, first thing for breakfast, before he eats any other food. (Then again, one parent told me when she tried this, her child *vomited* the broccoli. Which only goes to show, you have to do what works for you and your family!)
- Make sure your children are genuinely hungry at mealtimes. Mine still need snacks to avoid crabbiness, but I try to make sure the snacks are scheduled far enough away from lunch and dinner that they don't interfere with young appetites. If Mary isn't hungry at meals or snacks (she isn't, occasionally), we let her eat

as little as she likes. But no dessert is offered, and she's not allowed to eat anything else until the next meal or snack.

- Read and talk about nutrition so your children understand why you're changing their eating habits. Mine were fascinated by the lessons learned from *The Berenstain Bears and Too Much Junk Food:* soon afterward, Christian wanted "crunchy carrot sticks" every day, sometimes several times a day.
- Practice what you preach.

"I can't save money on groceries because I'm single and I eat out instead."

- Follow the basic guidelines that are outlined in the "Real-Life Shopping" chapter: set a limit on spending, compare prices, buy most groceries from the cheapest store, supplement by shopping at other stores whose weekly specials are outstanding, make a detailed shopping list. Then . . .
- Pre-prepare several meals at once. For example, on a night when you're fixing spaghetti, triple the recipe. Eat your fill, then package the rest in meal-size portions. Freeze for later meals.
- Buy fresh vegetables and freeze them. Eileen Duggan, a single friend of mine who shared several of these suggestions, prefers fresh corn on the cob (in the husk), brussel sprouts, green beans, and mushrooms (freeze uncooked); she says they're delicious reheated from the freezer. Or buy frozen vegetables in large bags, and cook only what you need for one meal.
- Eileen takes simple, nutritious lunches to work—like raw potatoes and acorn squash—for a quick fix in the microwave.
- Because she doesn't particularly like to shop, Eileen visits a farmers' market once a month for all her fruits and vegetables, Aldi once a month, and a discount supermarket if needed. She averages a total of a few hours, two to three shopping days each month. In this way, she spends little time buying food, has a well-stocked pantry on hand, and isn't as tempted to eat out.

"I can't save money on groceries because I can't be bothered with going to more than one grocery store."

- Then go to one, once a month, and do most of your shopping at a single time. Each *week's* grocery list should then be much

smaller, making a quick, weekly stop to your regular supermarket a manageable trip.
- "Beat the system" in that store.
- Try to buy only what's on sale, and stock up when you can.
- Ask the store meat manager about marked-down cuts of meat, and deli meat and cheese "ends." A friendly butcher can also offer good advice on bargain meats and ways to tenderize and cook them. Buy family-pack quantities, or ask the meat manager directly about purchasing 10 pounds-plus packages.
- Talk to the store produce manager about selling slightly damaged or bruised fruits and vegetables at half price.
- Have your friends and relatives call both the store meat manager and produce manager with the same requests. If enough people ask for discounted foods, supermarkets will usually try to oblige.
- Clip coupons religiously. Visit the store on double-coupon days.
- Buy all your meat for the month one week, all your canned and long-term supplies the next week, all your freezeable breads the next, most of your produce the next . . . you get the idea.

"I can't save money on groceries because I eat only high-priced natural, organic, whole foods."

- Then buy whole and natural foods through a co-op rather than a health food store. If there is currently no co-op in your area, contact the nearest food warehouse for information on how to organize one. See Resources, U.S. Cooperative Food Warehouses.
- Learn to cook most of your food from scratch, using ingredients you can control!
- Purchase meat directly from farmers you know and trust.
- Grow your own. Your Cooperative Extension Service agent will be glad to provide materials that show you how to garden organically.
- Process your own food through canning, freezing, drying, and pickling.
- Set up an informal cooperative with other friends, and take turns buying in bulk from produce wholesalers. You can scout out organic growers ahead of time.
- Buy from farmers' markets. Jill Bond, author of *Dinner's in the Freezer,* says she has found small farmers at these markets who

sell produce that's grown organically. From Jill's experience, these fruits and vegetables don't always cost extra.

- Call a local bartering exchange to find out if joining an exchange might enable you to trade with an organic foods supplier. See Resources, Organizations, and More.

"I can't save money on groceries because I have teenagers who eat me out of house and home!" (I asked the experts—parents of teens—for help on this one!)

- Then decide ahead of time what you'll make available for snacks and impromptu meals, and post it on the refrigerator. If your teen eats what isn't on the "OK To Eat" list, he pays for it, suggests Pat Edwards, author of *Cheap Eating,* or is penalized with extra chores.
- Keep sugary and/or junk foods out of the house. Instead, make sure there are plenty of nutritious foods—fresh fruits, veggies and dip, etc.—on hand.
- Have snacks waiting, near the door or on the kitchen table, when your teen walks into the kitchen. Everything should be already washed, diced, sliced, or otherwise prepared and ready to eat. The trick is to get him interested in what's convenient, rather than raiding the refrigerator and pantry, when he's starved.
- For meals, serve plenty of beans, whole grains, rice, pasta, casseroles, and soups, foods that are filling and healthful. One mother told me she buys 25-pound bags of whole wheat flour, and tries to always have homemade breads, muffins, waffles, and pancakes available for hungry young people.
- Involve your teenagers in gardening. They'll be more likely to eat produce when they've helped raise it. (A mother of 13 suggested this! Bet their garden was monstrous!)
- Keep a big pot of stew or chili simmering in the Crock-Pot® all weekend, says Mike Yorkey, author of *Saving Money Any Way You Can,* so in-and-out-the-door families always have an instant meal ready.
- Encourage your teens to help with shopping and cooking. Shopping gives them an idea of the cost of food, and also a chance to buy more expensive, favorite items with their own money if that particular food is not in your budget. Cooking helps ensure that there are foods around the house that teens especially like.

Then, in answer to the complaint, "There's nothing to eat here that I like," you can reply sweetly, "I have all the ingredients on hand for you to make your favorite banana bread!"

- Mega-cook®, so there are foods in your freezer available for snacks and quick meals. Use Jill Bond's once-every-six-months plan, or simply make several pizzas the next time you usually make one, and freeze the extras.

"I can't save money on groceries because I end up buying so many extra treats for birthdays and holidays."

- Then set a budget for birthdays and holidays and stick to it.
- Use your creativity—rather than your pocketbook—to make celebrations special. Buy a copy of *Baker's Easy Cut-Up Party Cakes,* for example, to learn how to assemble sensational cakes for next to nothing. See Resources.
- Stock up on food for birthday parties by purchasing ice cream, soda, and other treats on sale, using double coupons, if possible. (Hopefully we're all buying the low-fat, low-sugar versions, right? At least for the grown-ups?) Plan ahead.
- Bulk buy candy as party favors. Package it yourself.
- Understand, when dealing with children, that giving them everything money can buy is fulfilling a want, not a need.
- Compromise. Offer alternatives, such as a sleepover with VCR movies and homemade caramel corn, instead of a pizza party for 20. Is your child willing to finance an expensive party from his own savings?
- Give homemade gifts of food at Christmas time. See any of the December issues of thrift newsletters (listed in Resources) for excellent, low-cost ideas. Modify the recipes to make them healthier. Or assemble dry soup mixes with recipes attached. Bake whole grain breads and muffins. Share coupons for complete, to-be-delivered dinners.

"I can't save money on groceries because I don't see any need to do so."

- Then calculate how much you're spending on food right now. If your current weekly average is $100, and you cut back to $50, that's more than a $200 monthly savings, or $2,600 a year. (You

can also think of it as $2,600 of tax-free income.) Is there any-
thing else on which you would rather be spending this money?

"I can't save money on groceries because I just plain don't want to."

- Then . . . well, sorry. I don't have an answer for that one!

CHAPTER 6

Healthy, Low-Cost Recipes

Before plunging right into actual recipes, I must warn you about something I said in the beginning: I am not an outstanding cook. My purpose in including this chapter is certainly not to try and impress you with my culinary skills. Rather, I could imagine someone writing and saying something like, "You can't *really* make a yeast bread in 90 minutes total, can you? How do you do that?" Hopefully the following recipes will answer some of your questions in advance.

Many of these may almost seem an insult to advanced cooks. Doesn't everybody know how to make tuna salad, for heaven's sake? I used to think so, until meeting several individuals who had no idea how to do anything in the kitchen other than heat up a microwave dinner. So please bear in mind that some of the recipes are definitely geared toward beginners.

There are also some omissions. We Barfields eat nearly all of our fruits and vegetables plain and/or fresh, and so I've combined a few of our favorite cooked and combo "Vegetables" and "Salads" into a "Side Dishes" category. In "Meats and Main Dishes," you won't find entrees featuring expensive meat cuts; on $50 a week, who can afford it? There are also no fancy party foods here, or ones that take all day to prepare.

Most of the recipes included in this chapter are ones that I personally prepare. But for variety's sake, I've also added some that reflect other families' styles of cooking as well as their opinions of what it means to eat healthy. JoAnna Lund's desserts, for example, are all no-sugar (she uses artificial sweeteners), low-sodium, low-fat recipes. I've included desserts that use sugar in moderation, and some that use honey. Take your pick, according to your personal definition of what's good for *you*. Remember in the Introduction, when I told you about "the experts" disagreeing? Readers will, too, so I'm offering a variety of choices. You can balance out low-fat, low-calorie, and low-sugar dishes with richer desserts and side dishes. Serve a dinner that's high in protein one night, and the next, a vegetarian soup. You have all sorts of alternatives in this chapter.

At any rate, here are several recipes that have been helpful to me as I've learned to eat healthy for $50 a week.

Meats and Main Dishes

Baked Fruity Chicken

Serves 6

Source: Adapted from a recipe in *The $30 a Week Grocery Budget, Volume I,* by Donna McKenna.

Preheat oven to 350 degrees. Coat a 9 X 13 inch pan with nonstick baking spray. Place in the pan:

2 to 2½ pounds chicken pieces

Flip the pieces so both sides are coated. Top with:

Marmalade, preserves, or jelly, enough to lightly cover all chicken pieces

Bake for 45 to 50 minutes.

Variations: Sprinkle with any combination of salt, pepper, oregano, basil, rosemary, poultry seasoning, or paprika. *Or* pour tomato sauce over all the chicken pieces.

Tips: Donna recommends removing the chicken from the pan about 15 minutes before the meat is done, then filling the pan with a layer of cooked rice or cooked, cut-up potatoes. Place the chicken back on top and bake another 15 minutes. We've tried this and it's delicious.

Nutritional Data for One Serving (About 5 to 6 Ounces): Calories: 367, Calories from Fat: 181, Total Fat: 20g, Saturated Fat: 6g, Cholesterol: 162 mg, Sodium: 120 mg, Total Carbohydrate: 3g, Dietary Fiber: 0g, Sugars: 0g, Protein: 41g, Vitamin A: 29%, Vitamin C: 2%, Calcium: 2%, Iron: 14%

Beef and Noodle Soup

Serves 4

Source: *Healthy Exchanges Food Newsletter.**

1	full cup diced cooked lean roast beef (6 ounces)
½	cup chopped onion
1¾	cups canned beef broth (14½ ounce can)
2¼	cups water
⅛	teaspoon black pepper
¼	teaspoon minced garlic
1¾	cups uncooked noodles (3 ounces)
½	cup canned mushrooms, drained (2.5 ounce jar)
1	teaspoon dried parsley flakes

In a large saucepan sprayed with butter-flavored cooking spray, sauté diced roast beef and onion. Add beef broth, water, black pepper, and minced garlic. Bring mixture to a boil. Reduce heat. Simmer 10 minutes. Add noodles, mushrooms, and parsley flakes. Cover. Cook 10 minutes longer or until noodles are tender. Freezes well.

Serves 4 (1½ cups)
Each serving equals:
HE: 1½ Protein, 1 Bread, ½ Vegetable, 9 Optional Calories
205 Calories, 5 gm Fat, 17 gm Protein, 23 gm Carbohydrate, 492 mg Sodium, 3 gm Fiber
Diabetic: 1½ Meat, 1½ Starch

HINT: Purchase a chunk of roast beef from your local deli or a pkg of Healthy Choice sliced luncheon meats and dice either when you get home.

*Note: The format of this recipe differs from most recipes in this book at JoAnna Lund's—the author's—request that her original recipe remain exactly as it appeared in her newsletter.

Broiled Halibut in Soy Sauce

Serves 4 to 6

Source: A combination of several recipes recommended by Sally
Davis, seafood expert and friend.

Place in an ungreased 9 X 13 inch baking pan:

1 to 1½ pounds halibut steaks

Mix together:

¼   cup water
3   tablespoons lemon juice
2   tablespoons soy sauce
1   teaspoon ginger
¾   teaspoon grated lemon peel
½   teaspoon minced garlic

Pour liquid over fish. Cover and refrigerate for several hours. When
ready to eat, preheat oven to broil. Drain fish, reserving liquid. Place
fish on rack sprayed with nonstick cooking spray. Lightly coat fish
with reserved liquid. Broil five to seven minutes on each side, occasionally coating with extra liquid.

Variations: This recipe is delicious with other varieties of fish.
Try it with your latest catch!

Tips: Fish does not have to be marinated in advance if you're in
a hurry, but marinade does improve flavor.

Nutritional Data for One Serving (About 4 Ounces): Calories: 159, Calories
from Fat: 30, Total Fat: 3g, Saturated Fat: 0g, Cholesterol: 43mg, Sodium:
487mg, Total Carbohydrate: 2g, Dietary Fiber: 0g, Sugars: 0g, Protein: 29g,
Vitamin A: 6%, Vitamin C: 5%, Calcium: 7%, Iron: 7%

Cabbage Rolls

Serves 4 to 6

Source: My German friend, Anneliese Thomas,
and her expert advice!

Thoroughly wash:

1   medium-size head green cabbage

Remove brown or damaged leaves. Cut one inch off the bottom of the
cabbage and discard. Fill a large pan with:

2   cups water

Bring to a boil. Cook cabbage about 15 minutes, until leaves separate.
Drain cabbage in colander. Cool. In the meantime, brown in a large
frying pan:

6   ounces very lean ground beef or ground turkey
1   medium onion, chopped finely
2   cloves garlic, minced

Drain fat. Add:

1   cup tomato sauce
1   28-ounce can tomatoes
Salt and pepper to taste

Stir occasionally, and cook until onions are tender. Set aside. Pull 10
large outer leaves from cabbage and set aside. Dice remaining cabbage into small shreds, and add to meat mixture. Preheat oven to 375
degrees. Coat a shallow 9 X 13 inch baking pan with nonstick cooking spray.

Spread out large cabbage leaves on the counter. Using a slotted
spoon to dish up meat (and thus drain it somewhat), fill each leaf with
about ⅓ cup meat mixture. Fold right and left sides of the leaves
toward the middle, then roll from near to far. Secure each leaf with a
toothpick.

Place cabbage rolls in baking dish. Pour remaining sauce over
rolls. Cover with foil. Bake in preheated oven about one hour, or until
cabbage is tender.

Variations: Make a gravy rather than tomato sauce base: see Recipe Index for page number.

Tips: Be sure you cook the cabbage until it's *very* tender. I once made the mistake of shortening the boiling time: my cabbage was nearly raw, even after a long time in the oven! Add extra seasonings if you're cooking with ground turkey.

Nutritional Data for One Serving (2 Rolls): Calories: 173, Calories from Fat: 61, Total Fat: 7g, Saturated Fat: 2g, Cholesterol: 23mg, Sodium: 936mg, Total Carbohydrate: 20g, Dietary Fiber: 7g, Sugars: 12g, Protein: 12g, Vitamin A: 12%, Vitamin C: 222%, Calcium: 15%, Iron: 14%

Cheesy Tuna Garden Skillet

Serves 6

Source: *Healthy Exchanges Food Newsletter.**

1　(6 ounce) can white albacore tuna, packed in water, drained and flaked
1　(10¾ ounce) can Campbell's Healthy Request Cream of Mushroom soup
⅓　cup skim milk
¾　cup shredded Kraft reduced-fat Cheddar cheese (3 ounces)
¼　cup grated Kraft House Italian *or* Parmesan cheese (¾ ounce)
1　teaspoon dried parsley flakes
¼　teaspoon black pepper
2　cups canned sliced carrots, rinsed and drained (16 ounce can)
2　cups canned French-style green beans, rinsed and drained (16 ounce can)
2　cups cooked noodles

In a large skillet, combine tuna, mushroom soup, and skim milk. Stir in Cheddar cheese, House Italian cheese, parsley flakes, and black

*Note: The format of this recipe differs from most others in this book at JoAnna Lund's—the author's—request that her original recipe remain exactly as it appeared in her newsletter.

pepper. Mix well to combine. Cook over medium heat, stirring often, until cheese melts. Add carrots and green beans. Mix well to combine. Stir in noodles. Continue cooking, stirring often, until mixture is heated through. Freezes well.

Serves 6 (1 cup)
Each serving equals:
HE: 1⅓ Protein, 1⅓ Vegetable, ⅔ Bread, ¼ Slider, 13 Optional Calories
209 Calories, 5 gm Fat, 17 gm Protein, 24 gm Carbohydrate, 505 mg Sodium, 3 gm Fiber
Diabetic: 1½ Meat, 1½ Vegetable, 1 Starch

HINT: A full 1¾ cups dry noodles usually makes about 2 cups cooked.

Chicken, Bean, and Noodle Soup

Serves about as many as you need to serve

Source: A lot of odds-and-ends leftovers and a little creativity!

Combine in a Crock-Pot®:

All the leftover vegetables in your refrigerator that are less than four days old and/or smell OK and/or look OK, chopped into bite-size pieces
Any bits of meat or vegetables stored in the "soup bowl" in your freezer
Leftover pasta
Dabs of beans
Defatted meat broth *or* 3 to 4 bouillon cubes
Salt, pepper, garlic, and onion to taste
Enough water to cover it all

Cook 8 to 10 hours on low. Soup's on for supper!

Variations: See above! The sky's the limit! Instead of using a Crock-Pot®, simmer your soup on the stove until vegetables are tender.

Tips: My last soup—a very successful one—combined bits of cooked chicken, a few tablespoons of baked beans, some whole wheat noodles, and a little broccoli and corn. Sounds awful, but it was really good. See, you *can* use up leftovers!

Nutritional Data: Sorry, there's no way a nutritionist could analyze this one. Rest assured that if you keep the amount of meat small and use defatted broth, you'll have a healthy, delicious entree.

Chicken in Barbeque Sauce

Serves 6 to 8

Source: My dear mother.

Preheat oven to 350 degrees. Mix barbeque sauce together in a sauce-pan:

½   **cup chopped onion**
½   **cup ketchup**
⅓   **cup honey**
2   **teaspoons Worcestershire sauce**
    Dash of pepper

Cook over low heat for three minutes. Set aside. Coat the bottom of a nonstick frying pan with nonstick cooking spray. On medium-high heat, quickly brown:

2 to 3 pounds cut-up chicken pieces

Coat large casserole dish with nonstick cooking spray. Place seared chicken in dish. Cover with generous amounts of barbeque sauce. Bake for about an hour, or until tender.

Variations: Use barbeque sauce on pork, beef, turkey, or any other meat that happens to be on sale for the week.

Tips: Cook vegetables in the oven along with the meat, preferably on a layer below it in the same pan.

Nutritional Data for One Serving (5 to 6 Ounces): Calories: 372, Calories from Fat: 159, Total Fat: 18g, Saturated Fat: 5g, Cholesterol: 137mg, Sodium: 309mg, Total Carbohydrate: 17g, Dietary Fiber: 0g, Sugars: 2g, Protein: 35g, Vitamin A: 26%, Vitamin C: 11%, Calcium: 3%, Iron: 14%

Chili

Serves 6 to 8

Source: Several combined recipes, and plenty of experimenting.

Combine in a large metal saucepan:

2 **15-ounce cans red beans, liquid included**
1 **15-ounce can kidney beans, liquid included**
1 **large onion, finely chopped**
1 **green pepper, finely chopped**
¼ **cup molasses**
2 **teaspoons salt**
Chili powder to taste
Garlic powder to taste

Simmer for one to two hours, until flavors are well blended.
Serve topped with low-fat cheese and/or croutons.

Variations: Add leftover (lean) cooked meat of your choice. Discard liquid from beans and substitute one large can tomato or vegetable juice. Use canned tomatoes and extra seasoning in place of bean liquid. Substitute dry beans in place of canned beans for a better value; see package for cooking directions.

Tips: Cook in a Crock-Pot® for 8 hours or more; flavor improves with longer simmering time.

Nutritional Data for One Serving (About 1 Cup): Calories: 206, Calories from Fat: 8, Total Fat: 1g, Saturated Fat: 0g, Cholesterol: 0mg, Sodium: 1241 mg, Total Carbohydrate: 40g, Dietary Fiber: 10g, Sugars: 4g, Protein: 11g, Vitamin A: 6%, Vitamin C: 59%, Calcium: 15%, Iron: 29%

Enchilada Bake

Serves 6

Source: A recipe by Jan Kent, author of
A Taste of Dutch cookbook.

Preheat oven to 350 degrees. Brown in a frying pan:

½   **pound very lean ground beef or lean ground turkey**
1   **onion, finely chopped**
1   **carrot, grated**
1   **green or yellow pepper, finely chopped**

Add to the above mixture:

1   **large can Brooks Chili Hot Beans, drained**
1   **15-ounce can tomato sauce**

Cook until bubbly. Meanwhile, grate:

2   **cups low-fat mozzarella cheese**

Set aside. Open and set aside:

1   **package of 8 corn tortillas**

Coat a 9 X 13 inch baking pan with nonstick cooking spray. Layer
sauce mixture, mozzarella cheese, corn tortilla. Repeat until ingredients are all layered. Bake for 20 minutes, until heated through.

Variations: Replace meat mixture with all beans. Use dried
beans—instead of canned—and increase amounts of seasonings
used. Substitute store-bought taco seasoning mix for my recipe
below.

Tips: This dish is fast and really good. My two girls, who barely
tolerate beans, eat this one!

Nutritional Data for One Serving (About 1¼ Cups): Calories: 430, Calories
from Fat: 147, Total Fat: 16g, Saturated Fat: 7g, Cholesterol: 47mg, Sodium:
1285mg, Total Carbohydrate: 54g, Dietary Fiber: 5g, Sugars: 2g, Protein:
27g, Vitamin A: 60%, Vitamin C: 75%, Calcium: 40%, Iron: 26%

Taco Seasoning Mix

Combine:

 2 **teaspoons chili powder**
 2 **teaspoons dried parsley flakes**
 1½ **teaspoons cumin**
 1 **teaspoon paprika**
 1 **teaspoon onion salt**
 ½ **teaspoon oregano**
 ½ **teaspoon garlic powder**

This recipe is equivalent to a 1¼-ounce package of store-bought seasoning mix, and cheaper, especially if you buy spices in bulk and/or at a discount.

Enchiladas with Chicken

Serves 6

Source: Package directions on the tortillas, with a little
low-fat experimenting.

Dice:

 3 **cups cooked chicken**

Place in nonstick frying pan. Add:

 1 **cup water**
 1 **package taco seasoning mix**

Set aside. Shred:

 6 **cups lettuce**

Place in large bowl. Set aside. Grate:

 6 **ounces part-skim mozzarella (or other favorite low-fat) cheese**

Place in a bowl. Set aside. Dice:

 1 **large tomato**

Heat:

1   12-count package of flour or corn tortillas

in the oven or microwave according to package directions. Assemble on tortillas: cheese, hot meat mixture, lettuce, tomatoes. Fold bottom one-fourth of tortilla horizontally toward the top. Roll rest of tortilla vertically into a cylinder. Secure with toothpicks.

Variations: We usually assemble these enchiladas one at a time at the table. But sometimes I prepare several in advance, line them in a cake pan coated with nonstick cooking spray, spread a thin row of salsa and low-fat cheese on top, and bake for 10 minutes in a 400 degree oven. Any meat or bean mixture will substitute for chicken, but more seasoning is required for dried beans. I sometimes add leftover vegetables. Make your own taco seasoning mix, listed in previous recipe.

Tips: Tortillas can be made by hand but the process takes time. For a very similar taste, fry the store-bought version in a tiny bit of olive or canola oil.

Nutritional Data for One Serving (2 Enchiladas): Calories: 462, Calories from Fat: 151, Total Fat: 17g, Saturated Fat: 6g, Cholesterol: 81mg, Sodium: 891mg, Total Carbohydrate: 43g, Dietary Fiber: 1g, Sugars: 2g, Protein: 33g, Vitamin A: 15%, Vitamin C: 12%, Calcium: 31%, Iron: 24%

Frankfurter Special

Serves 6

Source: Adapted from a favorite recipe of my friend, JoAnn Knapp.

Preheat broiler. Combine in a saucepan:

1   tart medium apple, cored and diced
1   15-ounce can chunky pineapple
1   cup canned carrots
¼   cup water
1   chicken bouillon cube
1   tablespoon tomato juice

1   **tablespoon lemon juice**
½   **tablespoon cider vinegar**
⅛   **teaspoon ginger**

Place pan on burner over low heat. In the meantime, slice lengthwise, but not completely in two:

12   **turkey or chicken hot dogs**

Place in broiler and cook until hot dogs are heated through, about 3 minutes per side. While hot dogs are cooking, begin stirring liquid mixture, stirring frequently for about 10 minutes. Add broiled hot dogs and cook another 3 minutes.

Variations: JoAnn's original recipe called for ⅛ teaspoon cayenne pepper and ½ tablespoon curry powder added to the recipe above. Use fresh, diced carrots in place of cooked carrots.

Tips: We eat very few hot dogs, and so I've not tried this recipe. But I have a testimonial from JoAnn's two grown sons: this is still one of their all-time favorite dinners! For smaller children, you may want to cut up the hot dogs into tiny pieces before adding them to the liquid.

Nutritional Data for One Serving (2 Hot Dogs With Sauce): Calories: 268, Calories from Fat: 146, Total Fat: 16g, Saturated Fat: 5g, Cholesterol: 96mg, Sodium: 1353mg, Total Carbohydrate: 18g, Dietary Fiber: 1g, Sugars: 15g, Protein: 14g, Vitamin A: 34%, Vitamin C: 16%, Calcium: 11%, Iron: 12%

"Fried" Chicken

Serves 6

Source: An unidentified old clipping in my recipe file.

Preheat oven to 400 degrees. Line a 9 X 13 inch pan with foil, then place a wire rack on top. Coat the rack with nonstick cooking spray. Cut up:

1   **3–4 pound fryer (or 3 to 4 pounds of cut-up chicken)**

Wash chicken thoroughly with cold water. Pat dry. Set aside. In a small plastic bag, combine:

1   cup whole wheat bread crumbs, finely crumbled
¾   teaspoon onion powder
¾   teaspoon paprika
¾   teaspoon celery salt

Set aside. Brush chicken pieces with:

¼   cup plain nonfat yogurt

Shake the "spice bag" thoroughly, then dip chicken pieces, one at a time, into the bag. Place pieces on rack so they do not touch. Bake 45 to 50 minutes, until chicken is lightly browned and juices run clear when pierced with a fork.

Variations: Substitute cracker crumbs or corn flake crumbs for bread crumbs. Use any spice combination you like (no need to panic if you're out of celery salt).

Tips: Don't overcook the chicken or it becomes tough. Decide when it's finished by the fork test rather than the color test.

Nutritional Data for One Serving (About 8 Ounces): Calories: 470, Calories from Fat: 163, Total Fat: 18g, Saturated Fat: 10g, Cholesterol: 232mg, Sodium: 718mg, Total Carbohydrate: 14g, Dietary Fiber: 0g, Sugars: 0g, Protein: 62g, Vitamin A: 2%, Vitamin C: 1%, Calcium: 14%, Iron: 48%

Hamburger Stroganoff

Serves 6

Source: Adapted from a recipe in *The $30 a Week Grocery Budget, Volume I* by Donna McKenna.

Place a little water in a large frying pan. Sauté:

1   medium onion, finely chopped
1   clove garlic, crushed

Cook until limp. Add:

8   ounces cooked lean roast beef, cut into bite-size pieces
1½   cups water
5   beef bouillon cubes
      Salt and pepper to taste

Cover and cook. Meanwhile, place in a plastic container:

1½   tablespoons cornstarch
½   cup water

Cover with a tight-fitting lid. Shake vigorously until cornstarch is dissolved in liquid. Bring meat mixture to a boil. Add cornstarch and water mixture, stirring constantly until meat mixture boils again. Boil and stir for one more minute. Remove from heat. Add:

1   cup nonfat plain yogurt

Stir thoroughly. Serve over brown rice or whole wheat noodles.

Variations: Use whatever precooked meat you have on hand. The original recipe calls for hamburger. Add a can of (drained) mushrooms to the above ingredients.

Tips: You can substitute a can of cream of mushroom soup for the cornstarch and water mixture, but remember this drives up both the fat content and the cost.

Nutritional Data for One Serving (About 1 Cup Meat and Gravy): Calories: 131, Calories from Fat: 34, Total Fat: 4g, Saturated Fat: 1g, Cholesterol: 37mg, Sodium: 229mg, Total Carbohydrate: 7g, Dietary Fiber: 1g, Sugars: 3g, Protein: 16g, Vitamin A: 0%, Vitamin C: 4%, Calcium: 9%, Iron: 8%

Haystacks

Serves as many as you like!

Source: Adapted from a recipe by Jan Kent, author of
A Taste of Dutch cookbook.

"Stack" the following ingredients on each person's plate:

Crushed corn tortillas or reduced-fat corn chips
Cooked brown rice
Red chili beans (from a can or cooked dried beans)
Grated low-fat cheese
Chopped lettuce or greens
Chopped tomatoes
Diced onions
A few black olives

Top with:

Taco sauce or salsa
Nonfat Ranch dressing

Variations: This dish couldn't be more versatile, could it?!
Tips: If using dried beans (see Recipe Index), be sure to start preparing them the night before you serve Haystacks.

Nutritional Data: Too hard to figure!

Hazel's Five-Hour Stew

Serves 4 to 6

Source: Adapted from a recipe from my friend, Carol Haynes.

Preheat oven to 250 degrees. Place in a large, ovenproof casserole dish:

3   cups diced, uncooked chicken
6   carrots, sliced

2 **medium onions, diced**
½ **cup celery, sliced**
1 **small can peas, juice drained**
1 **12-ounce can tomato juice**
¾ **cup tomato paste**
¼ **cup water**
1½ **teaspoons salt**
1 **teaspoon sugar**
½ **teaspoon pepper**

Mix thoroughly. Cover casserole dish with a lid. Bake for five hours.

Variations: Simmer this stew in a Crock-Pot®, instead of in the oven, for 8 to 10 hours on low setting.

Tips: The original recipe calls for uncooked beef stew meat instead of chicken: by substituting chicken, you may find the stew too bland for your tastes. Sample it first, and add extra seasonings as needed.

Nutritional Data for One Serving (A Big Bowl): Calories: 295, Calories from Fat: 75, Total Fat: 8g, Saturated Fat: 2g, Cholesterol: 74mg, Sodium: 1345mg, Total Carbohydrate: 29g, Dietary Fiber: 7g, Sugars: 12g, Protein: 27g, Vitamin A: 260%, Vitamin C: 70%, Calcium: 8%, Iron: 20%

Italian Chicken and Angel Hair Pasta

Serves 6 to 8

Source: My own adaptation of a recipe shared by
my friend, JoAnn Knapp.

Prepare according to package directions:

16 **ounces angel hair pasta**

Set aside. Melt over medium heat in a large frying pan:

2 **tablespoons butter or margerine**

Add:

1   pound raw chicken, diced into bite-size pieces
1   small onion, diced
1   clove garlic, minced

Cook and stir until tender. Add a little water if needed. Drain. Stir in:

4   8-ounce cans tomato sauce
1   16-ounce can tomatoes
1   tablespoon Worcestershire *or* soy sauce
2   tablespoons Italian seasoning

Simmer, covered, stirring occasionally, for 10 to 15 minutes. Serve hot over pasta.

Variations: Any pasta will do; buy what's on sale! You can purchase spaghetti sauce in a jar instead of making your own from tomatoes, sauce, Worcestershire, and Italian seasoning.

Tips: To lower fat and calories even more, eliminate margarine and sauté chicken, onion, and garlic in a small amount of water.

Nutritional Data for One Serving (A Big Plateful!): Calories: 454*, Calories from Fat: 95, Total Fat: 11g, Saturated Fat: 2g, Cholesterol: 57mg, Sodium: 1002mg, Total Carbohydrate: 63g, Dietary Fiber: 2g, Sugars: 4g, Protein: 28g, Vitamin A: 23%, Vitamin C: 38%, Calcium: 8%, Iron: 31%

Lasagna

Serves 14 to 16

Source: My sister-in-law, Jane, came up with this winner.

Preheat oven to 400 degrees. Brown in a large frying pan:

1   pound extra-lean ground beef or ground turkey
1   large onion, chopped finely

Add and simmer for one hour:

2   15-ounce cans tomatoes
3   8-ounce cans tomato sauce

*Use reduced-fat margarine or butter and both calories and fat are reduced, too.

2 **tablespoons sugar**
1 **tablespoon Worcestershire sauce**
2 **tablespoons Italian seasoning**

Meanwhile, in a separate bowl, combine:

1 **pound small-curd, low-fat cottage cheese**
6 **egg whites**
½ **cup grated Parmesan cheese**

Prepare according to package directions:

1 **16-ounce package lasagna noodles**

Set aside. Grate and set aside:

1 **pound mozzarella cheese**

Coat two large 9 X 13 inch cake pans with nonstick cooking spray. Layer cooked noodles, cottage cheese mixture, mozarella cheese, and meat/tomato sauce, first in one pan, then the other. Bake for 45 minutes. Let stand for 10 minutes before serving.

Variations: Substitute your favorite spaghetti sauce for the tomato sauce mixture. Skip cooking the noodles, but make sure dry noodles are thoroughly covered with sauce; add a little extra water, then bake the dish at a slightly lower temperature, and a little longer than usual.

Tips: This recipe is expensive to make, but produces quite a lot of a very filling entree. It freezes well and actually improves in flavor after two days in the refrigerator. I often add more diced vegetables and decrease the amount of meat. (By the way, this is the same sauce from the recipe before, Italian Chicken and Angel Hair Pasta.)

Nutritional Data for One Serving (About 1 4″ Square): Calories: 345, Calories from Fat: 116, Total Fat: 13g, Saturated Fat: 6g, Cholesterol: 70mg, Sodium: 751mg, Total Carbohydrate: 32g, Dietary Fiber: 1g, Sugars: 5g, Protein: 25g, Vitamin A: 15%, Vitamin C: 23%, Calcium: 30%, Iron: 18%

Minestrone

Serves 4 to 6

Source: Adapted from a recipe in *Cheap Eating* by Pat Edwards.

Dice into bite-size pieces:

2 carrots
1 large onion
1 large potato

Set aside. Pour into large frying pan:

3 tablespoons canola oil

Heat. Add diced vegetables and sauté. Add:

1 can crushed tomatoes
5 cups water
    Rind of Parmesan cheese (or 2 ounces grated Parmesan cheese)

Let simmer for one hour.

Variations: Substitute one tablespoon tomato paste for the can of crushed tomatoes.

Tips: Cook this in your Crock-Pot® instead of on the stove.

Nutritional Data for One Serving (1 Bowl): Calories: 243, Calories from Fat: 105, Total Fat: 12g, Saturated Fat: 1g, Cholesterol: 8mg, Sodium: 402mg, Total Carbohydrate: 29g, Dietary Fiber: 3g, Sugars: 5g, Protein: 8g, Vitamin A: 93%, Vitamin C: 65%, Calcium: 19%, Iron: 11%

Momwiches

Serves 6 to 8

Source: Adapted from a recipe in *A Taste of Dutch* cookbook
by Jan Kent.

Brown in a large frying pan:

1   pound very lean ground beef or ground turkey

Sauté in a separate pan:

1   onion, diced
½   cup green pepper, diced
½   cup celery, diced
Enough water to just cover the bottom of the pan

Drain any grease from meat. Add diced vegetables. Also add:

1   cup ketchup
¼   cup vinegar
¼   cup brown sugar
1   teaspoon chili powder
½   teaspoon salt
½   teaspoon paprika
⅛   teaspoon pepper

Cover and simmer for 20 to 30 minutes. Serve on whole wheat buns
or bread.

Variations: You can simplify this recipe considerably by eliminating most of the vegetables and spices (though the taste won't be
the same, of course).

Tips: This recipe's taste is very similar to that of Manwiches®,
only much cheaper!

**Nutritional Data for One Serving (1 Generous Sandwich, With Meat Left
Over):** Calories: 239, Calories from Fat: 102, Total Fat: 11g, Saturated Fat:
4g, Cholesterol: 43mg, Sodium: 679mg, Total Carbohydrate: 23g, Dietary

Fiber: 2g, Sugars: 6g, Protein: 13g, Vitamin A: 7%, Vitamin C: 39%, Calcium: 3%, Iron: 11%

O'Brion's Irish Dish

Serves 8

Source: Adapted from a recipe in *The $30 a Week Grocery Budget, Volume II*, by Donna McKenna.

Preheat oven to 350 degrees. Cook in a frying pan over medium heat:

3   cups chicken, cut into bite-size pieces
½   cup defatted ham broth

Cook until chicken is tender, stirring occasionally. Set aside. Dice into bite-size pieces:

6   large potatoes, peeled
1   large onion
1   large green pepper

Coat a 9 X 13 inch baking pan with nonstick cooking spray. Mix chicken and vegetables, and place in pan. Bake for 40 to 45 minutes, until vegetables break easily with a fork.

Variations: The original recipe called for one package of Italian sausage. I discovered—by accident—that chicken cooked in ham broth tastes somewhat like sausage. But you can use whatever meat and/or broth you have on hand.

Tips: Add one-half of a package of onion soup mix if you'd like a more seasoned taste.

Nutritional Data for One Serving (A Large Plateful): Calories: 260, Calories from Fat: 45, Total Fat: 5g, Saturated Fat: 1g, Cholesterol: 46mg, Sodium: 100mg, Total Carbohydrate: 36g, Dietary Fiber: 4g, Sugars: 1g, Protein: 18g, Vitamin A: 3%, Vitamin C: 101%, Calcium: 3%, Iron: 13%

One-Dish Meal

Serves as many as you like!

Source: A newspaper column called "Wise Ways," by Linda
Blumenberg, a nutrition specialist (sorry, I have no date or address)
plus personal experience.

Here's another one of those totally flexible dishes, one that works
especially well with leftovers. Choose one item or combination of
items from each category below.

1½	**cups vegetables: mixed vegetables, tomatoes, corn, green beans, broccoli, peas, cabbage, and/or cooked and cubed acorn squash, zucchini, or potatoes**
1½ to 2	**cups chicken, fish, eggs, meat, dried beans or peas; canned tuna or other meat; cooked meat—like hamburger, turkey, chicken, pork, or lean sausage; hard-cooked egg, and/or cooked lentils, split peas, navy beans or pinto beans**
1 to 1½	**cups liquid ingredients: cheese or white sauce; cream soup, like mushroom, chicken, celery or broccoli; cheese soup; evaporated milk; tomato soup or sauce, or shredded cheese plus milk**
1 to 1½	**cups bread, rice or pasta; cubed bread, cooked macaroni, noodles, rice, spaghetti, barley, or bulgur**

Preheat oven to 325 degrees. Lightly coat a casserole dish with nonstick cooking spray. Combine all choices of ingredients above in a
large bowl. Add appropriate seasonings, such as sautéed garlic and/
or onion, salt, pepper, paprika, etc. Mix thoroughly. Place in casserole dish. If desired, add toppings such as bread crumbs, cracker
crumbs, or grated Parmesan cheese. Bake, covered, for 30 minutes.
Bake 15 minutes longer to brown topping.

Variations: Place ingredients in large skillet. Simmer, uncovered, on top of stove until bubbly.

Tips: Be sure the leftovers you use in this dish aren't spoiled: perishable leftovers in the refrigerator keep no longer than four days at most, according to Ms. Blumenberg, and leftover gravy and broth, no longer than two days. (If you store them in the freezer, your "safe" period extends to three months.)

Nutritional Data for One Serving: That really depends on what you put into this casserole!

Pizza

Serves 6

Source: This is my own recipe, and it's *good.*

Combine in a small bowl:

1	**cup very hot water**
2	**teaspoons yeast (or 2 packages)**

Mix thoroughly and set aside. In a larger bowl, combine:

2½	**cups white flour**
1½	**cups whole wheat flour**
1½	**teaspoons salt**
3	**tablespoons honey**
2	**tablespoons canola or olive oil**
2	**egg whites**

Add yeast mixture to flour mixture. Stir together until completely blended. Knead by hand for two minutes, adding flour as needed. Cover bowl with a clean dishcloth and set in a warm place. Let rise until doubled in size, about two to three hours. Divide dough into two mounds. Add enough flour to take the stickiness out of each mound, working flour into each mound. One at a time, on a floured surface, roll out dough to desired thickness. Add flour as needed. If dough is hard to roll, let stand for five minutes and try again.

Preheat oven to 400 degrees. Coat two large pizza pans with non-stick cooking spray and lightly flour. Place rolled pizza dough on pans. Layer on pizza:

Pizza sauce (see Variations)
Toppings of your choice (precooked very lean ground meat,

chopped green peppers, onions, mushrooms, etc.)
Part-skim mozzarella cheese, shredded

Bake for 12 to 20 minutes, depending on the thickness of your crust and desired crispness. Bottom should be lightly browned and cheese, bubbly.

Variations: You can make your own pizza sauce rather than buying store-bought. Combine and mix thoroughly:

2 **8-ounce cans tomato sauce**
½ **cup ketchup**
1 **tablespoon Italian seasoning**
Honey or sugar to taste

Tips: Skip the rising time if you're in a hurry; crust will be tougher.

Nutritional Data for One Serving (3 Large Slices): Calories: 777, Calories from Fat: 247, Total Fat: 27g, Saturated Fat: 11g, Cholesterol: 102mg, Sodium: 1115mg, Total Carbohydrate: 85g, Dietary Fiber: 7g, Sugars: 11g, Protein: 48g, Vitamin A: 22%, Vitamin C: 83%, Calcium: 41%, Iron: 40%

Poached Fish

Serves a versatile number

Source: My "seafood expert" and longtime friend, Sally Davis, and
a handout from Dixon's Cooking Classes.

Preheat oven to 400 degrees. Place in a large ovenproof pan:

"Meaty" fish (salmon, halibut, swordfish, or other fish that
will hold together while cooking) portions

Measure fish at the thickest part. Barely cover fish with:

Lightly salted water *or* water seasoned with herbs and
spices *or* milk (choose only one option)

*Carol Schlitt, Extension Educator who nutritionally analyzed this recipe, included one pound of ground beef in her analysis. To cut the fat content considerably (as we do), I use no more than *zero* to four ounces total for two pizzas.

Make sure oven is hot before fish goes in. Bake 10 minutes for every inch of thickness measured. Fish should flake easily.

Variations: Poached fish can be served hot, as an entree, with the sauce made by poaching. Or serve as the main ingredient of a casserole. Chilled and flaked, poached fish makes a delicious salad.

Tips: Eating fish is an important part of a healthy diet, but it can be expensive. Buy on sale, or go fishing, whenever you can!

Nutritional Data for One Serving (4 Ounces): Calories: 165, Calories from Fat: 37, Total Fat: 4g, Saturated Fat: 1g, Cholesterol: 42mg, Sodium: 102mg, Total Carbohydrate: 4g, Dietary Fiber: 0g, Sugars: 4g, Protein: 26g, Vitamin A: 10%, Vitamin C: 1%, Calcium: 15%, Iron: 6%

Pot "Pie"

Serves 6

Source: A recipe given us when Michael and I were first married
. . . 22 years ago!

Preheat oven to 350 degrees. Brown in a frying pan:

2   **cups diced chicken (raw, with a little water, or precooked)**
1   **small onion, diced**

When onion and chicken are both tender, add:

2   **cups green beans, liquid drained**
1   **8-ounce can tomato sauce**
1   **tablespoon Worcestershire sauce *or* soy sauce**
1   **teaspoon chili powder**
1   **teaspoon garlic**
½   **teaspoon salt**
¼   **teaspoon pepper**

Coat a large, ovenproof casserole dish with nonstick cooking spray. Pour mixture into casserole dish. Top with:

3   **cups mashed potatoes**

Bake for 30 minutes, until heated through.

Variations: If you prefer, add more chili powder. (We keep our dishes pretty bland, by some people's standards.)

Tips: When you're in a hurry, use instant mashed potatoes. We usually plan to serve this dish two days after we have mashed potatoes as a side dish: I just make twice the usual amount. (By the way, I think this entree was supposed to originally have a pie crust on the bottom of it, and that's why it's called "Pot Pie.")

Nutritional Data for One Serving (A Large Plateful and More): Calories: 204, Calories from Fat: 62, Total Fat: 7g, Saturated Fat: 2g, Cholesterol: 43mg, Sodium: 829mg, Total Carbohydrate: 21g, Dietary Fiber: 2g, Sugars: 1g, Protein: 16g, Vitamin A: 9%, Vitamin C: 22%, Calcium: 6%, Iron: 12%

Red Beans and Rice

Serves a large crowd

Source: Adapted from a recipe shared by Sally Davis.

Prepare:

2 pounds dry kidney beans

Sort through beans and eliminate "duds." In a large metal pan, cover beans with two inches of water and soak overnight.

The next day, drain liquid from beans. Set aside. Heat in a large frying pan:

2 tablespoons canola or olive oil

Over medium heat, stir in and cook until tender:

2 medium onions, diced
1 medium green pepper, diced
3 medium garlic cloves, minced

Add beans. Stir in:

1 small ham hock (or bits of ham)
1 16-ounce can diced tomatoes
1 tablespoon molasses or honey
2 bay leaves
½ teaspoon oregano
Salt, pepper, and red pepper to taste

Add:

Enough water to cover everything in the pan.

Bring to a boil. Reduce heat and simmer until beans are tender. Serve over brown rice.

Variations: Eliminate the ham hock and add more seasonings for a vegetarian dish. Substitute canned kidney beans for dried ones. The original recipe calls for smoked sausage (stirred in during the last 20 minutes of cooking), plus ½ teaspoon dried marjoram, and ½ teaspoon dried thyme.

Nutritional Data for One Serving Rice and Beans (A Big, Big Bowl!): Calories: 545, Calories from Fat: 71, Total Fat: 8g, Saturated Fat: 1g, Cholesterol: 2mg, Sodium: 301mg, Total Carbohydrate: 99g, Dietary Fiber: 4g, Sugars: 4g, Protein: 22g, Vitamin A: 4%, Vitamin C: 41%, Calcium: 16%, Iron: 38%

Salmon Croquettes

Serves 4 to 6

Source: My dear mother.

Combine in a bowl:

1	**15-ounce can salmon**
1	**8-ounce can water-packed tuna**
2	**egg whites**
¼	**cup nonfat milk**
1	**cup crushed saltine crackers**

Preheat oven to broil setting. Debone salmon and discard most of the liquid. Drain and discard liquid from tuna. Mix ingredients, and shape mixture into small patties. Crush additional cracker crumbs and roll the patties in extra crumbs. Broil for about 10 minutes on one side, until nicely browned. Turn, and broil an additional 6 to 8 minutes. Croquettes should be crispy.

Variations: You can stretch the salmon mixture by changing this recipe as follows: add two slices of finely shredded whole wheat bread, two more egg whites, and enough liquid (milk and/or salmon juice) to moisten. Broil as usual. We sometimes fry the croquettes in canola oil.

Tips: If canned salmon is outrageously expensive, try using all tuna, but be prepared for a less tasty entree. This recipe is a favorite with my children.

Nutritional Data for One Serving (2 to 3 Croquettes): Calories: 290, Calories from Fat: 84, Total Fat: 9g, Saturated Fat: 2g, Cholesterol: 55mg, Sodium: 855mg, Total Carbohydrate: 19g, Dietary Fiber: 0g, Sugars: 1g, Protein: 32g, Vitamin A: 3%, Vitamin C: 0%, Calcium: 24%, Iron: 15%

Saucy "Faux" Steaks

Serves 6

Source: *Healthy Exchanges Food Newsletter.**

16	oz ground 90% lean turkey or beef
6	tablespoons dried bread crumbs (1½ ounces)
¼	cup finely chopped onion
½	cup Healthy Choice ketchup
1¾	cups canned stewed tomatoes with juice (14½ ounce can)

In a large bowl, combine meat, bread crumbs, onion and ¼ cup ketchup. Mix well. Using a full ⅓ cup measure as a guide, form into six patties. Place patties in a large skillet sprayed with butter-flavored cooking spray. Brown on both sides. In a small bowl, combine stewed tomatoes and remaining ¼ cup ketchup. Pour mixture evenly over meat. Lower heat. Cover and simmer 15 minutes. For each serving, place piece of "steak" on plate and evenly spoon sauce over top. Freezes well.

Serves 6
Each serving equals:

*Note: The format of this recipe differs from most others in this book at JoAnna Lund's—the author's—request that her original recipe remain exactly as it appeared in her newsletter.

HE: 2 Protein, ⅔ Vegetable, ⅓ Bread, ½ Slider
175 Calories, 7 gm Fat, 15 gm Protein, 13 gm Carbohydrates, 475 mg Sodium
Diabetic: 2 Meat, 1 Vegetable, ½ Starch

HINT: Good served with rice, pasta or potatoes.

Spaghetti

Serves 6

Source: My own cozy kitchen.

Prepare according to package directions:

16   ounces spaghetti or similar pasta

Set aside. Combine in a large frying pan:

3   8-ounce cans tomato sauce
1   16-ounce can tomatoes, crushed
2   tablespoons Italian seasoning
1   tablespoon molasses

Simmer for about 30 minutes, until mixture is thick and bubbly. Serve hot over spaghetti.

Variations: Add diced meat to spaghetti sauce.
Tips: Spaghetti can be brought to a boil, covered immediately, heat turned off, then left to stand for a couple hours. The pasta will finish cooking itself.

Nutritional Data for One Serving (2 Medium Plates, Filled): Calories: 347, Calories from Fat: 15, Total Fat: 2g, Saturated Fat: 0g, Cholesterol: 0mg, Sodium: 871mg, Total Carbohydrate: 72g, Dietary Fiber: 2g, Sugars: 4g, Protein: 12g, Vitamin A: 21%, Vitamin C: 36%, Calcium: 10%, Iron: 32%

Steamed Fish in Foil

Serves 6

Source: Adapted from a recipe shared by Sally Davis.

Preheat oven to 400 degrees. Cut six 12-inch squares of aluminum foil. Place in the center of each square:

- 1 **4-ounce fillet of turbot or other white-fleshed fish (24 ounces total)**
- 1 **large mushroom (6 total), sliced**
- 2 **thin slices of onion (1 medium onion total)**
- ½ **tablespoon fresh chopped dill (3 tablespoons total)**
- 1 **tablespoon water (about ¾ cup total)**
- **Salt and black pepper**

Measure fish fillet at thickest part. Turn foil edges upward to create a cup. Seal top of foil completely shut. Place foil packets on baking sheet. Bake in preheated oven, allowing 10 minutes for each inch of thickness (round it out to the nearest inch, average).

Variations: Add thinly sliced potatoes and carrots, precooked in the microwave.

Tips: Open the foil packets carefully: the steam can burn you!

Nutritional Data for One Serving (1 Packet): Calories: 122, Calories from Fat: 31, Total Fat: 3g, Saturated Fat: 0g, Cholesterol: 54mg, Sodium: 527mg, Total Carbohydrate: 3g, Dietary Fiber: 1g, Sugars: 1g, Protein: 19g, Vitamin A: 1%, Vitamin C: 7%, Calcium: 3%, Iron: 4%

Stir-Fry

Serves 6 to 8

Source: My own experimenting.

Slice into thin strips:

- 4 **cups carrots, onions, zucchini, cucumbers, sweet potatoes, broccoli, and/or other fresh produce**

Set aside. In a large nonstick frying pan, heat:

1   tablespoon olive or canola oil

When oil is hot enough to sizzle a drop of water, quickly sauté vegetables to desired doneness. Stir in:

2   tablespoons soy sauce
2   tablespoons chunky peanut butter
2   cloves garlic, finely minced

Simmer. Combine in an airtight plastic bowl:

2   tablespoons cornstarch
1   cup water

Shake the cornstarch and water together until smooth. Add to vegetables. Bring to a boil, stirring constantly, for one minute. Turn down heat and add a small amount of cooked leftover chicken. Serve hot over brown rice.

Variations: I like to use this recipe when I'm ready to clean up leftovers, as you can toss in nearly anything on hand. It's not as Oriental with green beans and potatoes, of course, but still tastes good. Most kinds of meat or combinations of meats, used very sparingly, work well, or meat can be left out entirely.

Tips: To cut down on fat even more, eliminate the peanut butter.

Nutritional Data for One Serving (A Big Plateful): Calories: 266, Calories from Fat: 53, Total Fat: 6g, Saturated Fat: 1g, Cholesterol: 0mg, Sodium: 349mg, Total Carbohydrate: 48g, Dietary Fiber: 5g, Sugars: 4g, Protein: 6g, Vitamin A: 88%, Vitamin C: 29%, Calcium: 5%, Iron: 8%

Susan Thomas's Casserole

Serves 12 to 15

Source: Adapted from a recipe in *Dinner's in the Freezer*
by Jill Bond.

Brown in a large frying pan:

1½   pounds ground chuck or ground turkey
1   cup onion, chopped

When meat is cooked and onions are tender, drain grease. Preheat oven to 350 degrees. Prepare according to package directions:

1   10-ounce package noodles

Set aside. Add to meat and onion mixture:

1   16-ounce can corn
1   can cream of chicken soup
1   can cream of mushroom soup
1   cup nonfat yogurt
¼   cup chopped pimento
1½ teaspoon salt
½   teaspoon pepper
    Cooked noodles

Mix thoroughly. Pour into two medium-size, ovenproof casserole dishes. Bake for 30 minutes.

Variations and Tips: Jill mega-cooks®, so her basic recipe (above) yields two meals (12 to 15 servings). She goes further in each of her recipes, as in this one, when she increases the yield to *six* meals. The ingredients are:

1   family pack of ground turkey or beef
       (approximately 10 to 12 pounds)
5 to 6 cups chopped onions
1   #10 can kernel corn, drained
2   large cans (26 ounces) cream of chicken soup
2   large cans (26 ounces) cream of mushroom soup
1   large carton (3 pounds) sour cream (I changed this
       to nonfat yogurt)
1   large package (40 ounces) cooked noodles

Instructions are the same until after the ingredients are mixed: at that point, everything's divided into six casserole dishes, labeled, carefully wrapped and frozen (before cooking). Each dish is thawed before serving, then baked.

Nutritional Data for One Serving (A Generous Plateful): Calories: 276, Calories from Fat: 106, Total Fat: 12g, Saturated Fat: 4g, Cholesterol: 45mg, Sodium: 856mg, Total Carbohydrate: 29g, Dietary Fiber: 1g, Sugars: 2g, Protein: 15g, Vitamin A: 23%, Vitamin C: 145%, Calcium: 7%, Iron: 78%

Sweet 'n' Sour Meatballs

Serves 8 to 10

Source: Adapted from a recipe in *Dinner's in the Freezer*
by Jill Bond.

Mix together in a large bowl:

2   pounds lean ground beef or ground turkey
2   egg whites
Salt, pepper, onion salt, and garlic powder, as desired

Form mixture into one inch balls (try to get 32 to 40 from two pounds
of meat). Brown meatballs in a large nonstick skillet until "done."
Drain grease. Set aside. In a small pan, sauté in a little water until
tender:

1   green pepper, cut into 1-inch strips

Set aside. Open:

2   cans (16-ounce) chunk pineapple

Drain pineapple, reserving liquid in a water-tight plastic container.
Add to this container:

2   tablespoons cornstarch or flour

Put lid on container and shake vigorously until lumps are gone. Pour
liquid into another saucepan. Add:

4   tablespoons vinegar (white or cider)
2   tablespoons sugar (white or brown)
1   tablespoon soy sauce

Bring to a boil, stirring constantly, until sauce becomes thick. Combine meatballs, pineapple chunks, green pepper, and sauce in the
original large skillet (the one you used to cook the meat). Heat
through.

Variations: Jill uses granulated fructose instead of sugar. She
also adds raw green peppers to the recipe rather than sautéeing them
first.

Tips: If sauce seems too thick, thin with a little juice or water. My family *loves* this recipe!

Nutritional Data for One Serving (4 Meatballs): Calories: 325, Calories from Fat: 156, Total Fat: 17g, Saturated Fat: 7g, Cholesterol: 67mg, Sodium: 661mg, Total Carbohydrate: 23g, Dietary Fiber: 1g, Sugars: 18g, Protein: 20g, Vitamin A: 2%, Vitamin C: 54%, Calcium: 3%, Iron: 14%

Tuna Salad

Serves 4 to 6

Source: Adapted from my mother's recipe.

Combine in a bowl:

1   **large can water-packed tuna**
2   **hard-boiled eggs, yolks discarded, diced**
4   **tablespoons nonfat or low-fat mayonnaise**
1   **tablespoon sweet relish**
1   **tablespoon sugar**

Chill thoroughly. Serve on oven-toasted whole wheat buns or French bread.

Variations: Add extra nonfat mayonnaise if a creamier texture is desired. Substitute diced chicken or turkey for tuna. Substitute all egg whites for meat, and add ½ teaspoon paprika.

Tips: Serve stuffed in peppers, celery, or tomatoes.

Nutritional Data for One Serving (Enough to Fill a Sandwich): Calories: 111, Calories from Fat: 33, Total Fat: 4g, Saturated Fat: 0g, Cholesterol: 19mg, Sodium: 231mg, Total Carbohydrate: 4g, Dietary Fiber: 0g, Sugars: 2g, Protein: 14g, Vitamin A: 1%, Vitamin C: 0%, Calcium: 1%, Iron: 5%

Turkey Broccoli Casserole

(Read the entire page before you begin to cook!)

Serves 6 to 8

Source: Adapted from a recipe shared by Anneliese Thomas.

Here's the traditional recipe. Notice how I change it in the second half of the page.

Preheat oven to 350 degrees. Combine in a saucepan:

1   **can cream of chicken soup**
1   **cup chicken or turkey broth**
1   **8-ounce package Velveeta cheese**

Heat, stirring occasionally, until cheese melts. Set aside. In a separate saucepan, cook until almost tender:

1   **package frozen broccoli**

Set aside. Dice into small pieces:

1 to 2 cups leftover turkey

Set aside. In a bowl, prepare:

1   **package stuffing mix**

Place in a greased casserole dish as follows: diced turkey, broccoli, cheese sauce. Top with stuffing. Bake for 20 to 30 minutes, until cheese bubbles and stuffing is lightly browned on top.

Variations and Tips: This recipe can be easily altered to save money and increase nutrition, with little additional time required. Here's my version of the casserole:

Shake together in an airtight container:

1   **cup skim milk**
3   **tablespoons flour**
Dash of salt and pepper

Heat in a saucepan, stirring until bubbly. Add:

½ **cup low-fat mozzarella cheese, shredded**
2 **tablespoons soy sauce *or* 2 tablespoons Worcestershire
sauce**

Cook and stir just until smooth and thickened. Set aside. Steam until
tender:

1 **medium head fresh broccoli, diced**

Dice:

1 **cup cooked turkey**

Place in a nonstick casserole dish as follows: diced turkey, broccoli,
cheese sauce. Top with:

2 **cups homemade croutons**

Bake for 20 to 30 minutes, until cheese bubbles and stuffing is lightly
browned on top.

It's cheaper, it's healthier, and it takes about five more minutes to
assemble than the original recipe!

Nutritional Data for One Serving (Based on My Version, About 1 Cup): Calories:
125, Calories from Fat: 23, Total Fat: 3g, Saturated Fat: 1g, Cholesterol:
19mg, Sodium: 475mg, Total Carbohydrate: 13g, Dietary Fiber: 2g, Sugars:
2g, Protein: 12g, Vitamin A: 10%, Vitamin C: 28%, Calcium: 8%, Iron: 7%

Turkey Burgers

Serves 8

Source: Adapted from a recipe in *Cheap Eating* by Pat Edwards.

Combine in a large bowl:

1 **pound ground turkey**
4 **egg whites**
½ **cup dry oats**
⅓ **cup ketchup**
1 **medium onion, finely chopped**
1 **teaspoon garlic powder**

Form into patties. "Fry" in a skillet coated generously with nonstick cooking spray, until nicely browned.

Variations: When trying this recipe, I broiled the burgers rather than frying them. I also omitted the rest of the original recipe, which you may want to include.

Flip and place on each burger:

1 **slice Swiss cheese (8 total)**

Mix together:

2 **tablespoons horseradish**
½ **cup (nonfat) mayonnaise**

Spread mayo mix on a rye bread or bun and top with a burger.

Tips: I once used this recipe to make meat loaf. I coated muffin pans with nonstick cooking spray, added enough meat to fill each cup, and baked them in a 400 degree oven for about 25 minutes. We liked the "meat loaf cups" even better than the burgers!

Nutritional Data for One Serving (1 Burger): Calories: 136, Calories from Fat: 50, Total Fat: 6g, Saturated Fat: 1g, Cholesterol: 45mg, Sodium: 68mg, Total Carbohydrate: 8g, Dietary Fiber: 2g, Sugars: 1g, Protein: 13g, Vitamin A: 0%, Vitamin C: 2%, Calcium: 2%, Iron: 7%

Vegetable Beef Soup

Serves 6 to 8

Source: Adapted from a Crock-Pot® recipe book.

Combine in a Crock-Pot®:

1 **15-ounce can tomatoes**
2 **carrots, sliced**
2 **stalks celery, sliced**
2 **medium onions, diced**
2 **medium potatoes, peeled and diced**
3 **cups water**
1 **teaspoon salt**
4 **whole peppercorns**
3 **beef bouillon cubes**

Cover and cook on low for 12 to 24 hours.

Variations: Use this soup as a catch-all for whatever is in your freezer or refrigerator. The last time I made it, I added leftover ham broth, a little broccoli, a can of green beans, one frozen tomato, and some odds-and-ends vegetables to the ingredients above. Instead of a Crock-Pot®, combine the ingredients in a large kettle, and simmer on the stove all afternoon.

Tips: Serve topped with homemade croutons (see Recipe Index).

Nutritional Data for One Serving (2 Bowls): Calories: 105, Calories from Fat: 3, Total Fat: 0g, Saturated Fat: 0g, Cholesterol: 0mg, Sodium: 429mg, Total Carbohydrate: 22g, Dietary Fiber: 3g, Sugars: 4g, Protein: 5g, Vitamin A: 62%, Vitamin C: 46%, Calcium: 4%, Iron: 6%

Breads and Breakfast Foods

Bagels

Makes 12 bagels

Source: Adapted from a recipe in *Cheap Eating* by Pat Edwards.

Mix, until dissolved, in a large bowl:

⅔   **cup very warm water**
5   **teaspoons dry yeast (or 2 packages)**

Add:

1   **cup whole wheat flour**
1   **cup white flour**
¾   **cup water**
2   **tablespoons honey**
1   **tablespoon salt**

Mix ingredients on high speed of electric mixer for two minutes. Reduce speed and gradually add:

2   **cups white flour**

When the dough becomes stiff, turn onto a floured board and knead by hand (or use a dough hook) until smooth. Place in a bowl lightly coated with nonstick cooking spray. Cover and let rest for 15 minutes. Divide dough into 12 balls. Pierce the center of each ball to make the center hole. Pull to enlarge. Let rise, covered, for 30 minutes on a baking sheet lightly coated with nonstick cooking spray. Preheat oven to 375 degrees. In a large saucepan, bring to a boil:

4   **quarts water**
1   **teaspoon sugar**

Reduce heat to simmer and add four bagels. After three minutes, turn and simmer four minutes longer. Remove. Pat dry and place on lightly sprayed baking sheet. Repeat with the remaining bagels. Bake for 30 minutes.

Variations: Add cinnamon *or* onion flakes to the bagel dough (not both!).

Tips: These take time, but are really delicious, much better than storebought. The next time we make them, I intend to make a huge batch and freeze a few.

Nutritional Data for One Serving (1 Bagel): Calories: 165, Calories from Fat: 5, Total Fat: 1g, Saturated Fat: 0g, Cholesterol: 0mg, Sodium: 535mg, Total Carbohydrate: 35g, Dietary Fiber: 2g, Sugars: 3g, Protein: 5g, Vitamin A: 0%, Vitamin C: 0%, Calcium: 1%, Iron: 11%

Banana Bread

Makes 3 thin loaves, about 10 slices per loaf

Source: Lyn Hoeft, long-time friend, shared this recipe with me,
and I took the fat out!

Preheat oven to 350 degrees. Coat three loaf pans with nonstick cooking spray, then lightly flour.

Cream together in a large bowl:

1	**cup sugar**
8	**very ripe bananas, diced**
8	**egg whites**

In a separate bowl, sift together:

1¼	**cups white flour**
1	**cup whole wheat flour**
2	**teaspoons baking soda**
1	**teaspoon salt**

Combine flour mixture with creamed mixture and blend thoroughly. Turn into pans. Bake for 40 to 50 minutes.

Variations: Add nuts and/or raisins.

Tips: Check for doneness by inserting a toothpick in three or four areas of the bread; if you go through a piece of banana, you may sink into a gooey spot and think the bread isn't done.

Nutritional Data for One Serving (1 Slice): Calories: 92, Calories from Fat: 3, Total Fat: 0g, Saturated Fat: 0g, Cholesterol: 0mg, Sodium: 170mg, Total Carbohydrate: 21g, Dietary Fiber: 1g, Sugars: 11g, Protein: 2g, Vitamin A: 0%, Vitamin C: 5%, Calcium: 1%, Iron: 3%

Banana-Cranberry Muffins

Serves 8

Source: *Healthy Exchanges Food Newsletter.**

1½ cups flour
1 (4 serving) pkg Jell-O sugar-free instant banana pudding mix
¼ cup Sprinkle Sweet *or* Sugar Twin
1 teaspoon baking powder
1 teaspoon baking soda
½ teaspoon JO's Apple Pie Spice**
1 cup chopped fresh cranberries
⅔ cup mashed bananas (2 ripe medium)
1 teaspoon vanilla extract
2 eggs *or* equivalent in egg substitute
½ cup unsweetened applesauce

Preheat oven to 350 degrees. In a large bowl, combine flour, dry pudding mix, Sprinkle Sweet, baking powder, baking soda and JO's Apple Pie Spice. Add chopped cranberries. Mix well. In a small bowl, combine mashed bananas, vanilla extract, eggs and applesauce. Add banana mixture to flour mixture. Mix just until combined. Spray muffin tins with butter-flavored cooking spray or line with muffin liners. Fill muffin wells. Bake 22 to 25 minutes or until muffins test done. Cool on wire rack. Freezes well.

Serves 8
Each serving equals:

*Note: The format of this recipe differs from most others in this book at JoAnna Lund's—the author's—request that her original recipe remain exactly as it appeared in her newsletter.
**See Resources, "Miscellaneous Products and Videos," on how to order JO's Spices.

HE: 1 Bread, ¾ Fruit, ¼ Protein (limited), 19 Optional Calories
154 Calories, 2gm Fat, 4gm Protein, 30gm Carbohydrate, 325 mg Sodium, 2 gm Fiber
Diabetic: 1 Starch, 1 Fruit

HINT: 1) Substitute any reputable brand for JO's Apple Pie Spice. 2) Fill unused muffin wells with water. It protects the muffin tin and ensures even baking.

Breadsticks

Fills a small basket, about 24 sticks total

Source: Unknown.

Preheat oven to 350 degrees. Spread several slices of whole wheat bread on a cookie sheet. Sprinkle on garlic powder, minced onion, paprika, or any other seasonings you enjoy. Cut each slice into five or six narrow rectangles. Bake for about 10 minutes, or until bottom side is browned; turn over and bake another 5 to 10 minutes. Serve hot or cold.

Nutritional Data for One Serving (1 Stick): Calories: 14, Calories from Fat: 2, Total Fat: 0g, Saturated Fat: 0g, Cholesterol: 0mg, Sodium: 25mg, Total Carbohydrate: 3g, Dietary Fiber: 0g, Sugars: 0g, Protein: 1g, Vitamin A: 1%, Vitamin C: 0%, Calcium: 0%, Iron: 1%

Croutons

Fills a quart jar, about 16 servings

Source: Unknown again.

Preheat oven to 350 degrees. Dice into small cubes:

8   slices thick bread

Place in a large bowl. Sprinkle on:

Garlic powder, minced onion, paprika, and/or other seasonings, as desired

Coat bread cubes lightly with nonstick cooking spray. Toss gently. Turn onto nonstick cookie sheet. Bake for 20 to 30 minutes, stirring occasionally, until crisp.

Variations: Experiment with several seasonings until you find a taste your family loves.

Tips: Slightly dry bread works a little better than fresh. I keep a plastic bag in the freezer for storing bread ends and leftovers; when the bag is full, I have just enough for a batch of breadsticks or croutons.

Nutritional Data for One Serving (About ½ Slice of Bread): Calories: 41, Calories from Fat: 7, Total Fat: 1g, Saturated Fat: 0g, Cholesterol: 0mg, Sodium: 75mg, Total Carbohydrates: 8g, Dietary Fiber: 0g, Sugars: 0g, Protein: 2g, Vitamin A: 3%, Vitamin C: 1%, Calcium: 1%, Iron: 3%

Breakfast Biscuits

Serves 8

Source: *Healthy Exchanges Food Newsletter.*[*]

1½   **cups Bisquick reduced-fat baking mix**
¼   **cup + 1 tablespoon Sprinkle Sweet *or* Sugar Twin**
½   **cup raisins**
¼   **cup Kraft fat-free mayonnaise**
¾   **cup water**
½   **teaspoon cinnamon**

Preheat oven to 415 degrees. In a medium bowl, combine baking mix, ¼ cup Sprinkle Sweet and raisins. Add mayonnaise and water. Mix well to combine. Spray muffin tin with butter-flavored cooking spray. Fill 8 wells half full. In a small bowl, combine remaining one tablespoon Sprinkle Sweet and cinnamon. Evenly sprinkle mixture over biscuit. Cut mixture into biscuit with a knife. Bake 10 to 12 minutes. Cool on wire rack. Freezes well.

*Note: The format of this recipe differs from most others in this book at JoAnna Lund's—the author's—request that her original recipe remain exactly as it appeared in her newsletter.

Serves 8
Each serving equals:
HE: 1 Bread, ½ Fruit, 9 Optional Calories
126 Calories, 2 gm Fat, 2 gm Protein, 25 gm Carbohydrate, 304 mg Sodium,
1 gm Fiber
Diabetic: 1 Starch, ½ Fruit

HINT: 1) Fill unused muffin wells with water. It protects the muffin tins and
ensures even baking.
2) Leftovers freeze well.

Cinnamon Yeast Bread (90-Minute Bread)

Makes 4 loaves

Source: A recipe from a neighbor of 22 years ago,
plus my own adaptations.

Dissolve together in a small, shallow bowl:

1   **cup very warm water**
4   **packages (or 3 tablespoons) yeast***

Set aside. In a large bowl, combine:

3   **cups very warm water**
4   **teaspoons salt**
3   **tablespoons honey**
4   **tablespoons olive or canola oil**

Combine the two mixtures. Stir in thoroughly:

4   **cups whole wheat flour**
5   **cups white flour**

Add extra flour a little at a time, just enough to form a soft dough.
*Knead by pounding dough vigorously with a large spoon for one
minute.* (This is not a mistake!) Form four mounds of dough and let

*This is a lot of yeast, I know, but that's what makes the bread rise so quickly.
If you don't mind a longer rising time, you can use half the amount of yeast.

stand. One at a time, roll out each mound with a rolling pin on a floured surface to form a rectangle. Sprinkle on each rectangle:

1   tablespoon brown sugar (4 tablespoons total)
½   teaspoon cinnamon (2 teaspoons total)

Start at one of the long ends of each rectangle and roll up tightly to form compact loaves. Tuck loose ends under, seam sides down. Place in four bread pans coated with nonstick cooking spray. Let rise, covered in a warm place, for 30 minutes. Bake in preheated 350 degree oven for 30 to 40 minutes.

Variations: This bread can be baked as plain whole wheat bread by eliminating the rolling-out procedure. Simply smooth out the dough and place it directly into pans for rising.

Tips: This is one of our favorite recipes, absolutely delicious! From start to finish takes only 90 minutes or less. It is sometimes difficult to tell when the bread is really done, and you may have to actually cut a loaf in half to make sure there are no doughy areas. Extra loaves freeze well.

Nutritional Data for One Serving (1 Slice): Calories: 122, Calories from Fat: 17, Total Fat: 2g, Saturated Fat: 0g, Cholesterol: 0mg, Sodium: 215mg, Total Carbohydrates: 23g, Dietary Fiber: 2g, Sugars: 1g, Protein: 4g, Vitamin A: 0%, Vitamin C: 0%, Calcium: 1%, Iron: 8%

Corn Bread (Muffins)

Serves 12

Source: Adapted from a recipe in *A Taste of Dutch* cookbook
by Jan Kent.

Preheat oven to 400 degrees. Mix together:

2   cups cornmeal
1   cup whole wheat flour
1   cup white flour
¾   cup dry milk powder
4   tablespoons brown sugar
6   teaspoons baking powder
1   teaspoon salt

Set aside. In another bowl, mix together:

6 **beaten egg whites**
2 **cups skim milk**
¼ **cup applesauce**
¼ **cup canola or olive oil**

Add wet ingredients to dry ingredients, stirring just until smooth. Do not beat. Pour into a 9 X 13 inch pan coated with nonstick cooking spray. Bake for 25 to 30 minutes.

Variations: To make muffins, pour corn bread into muffin tins coated with nonstick cooking spray. Bake for about 15 to 20 minutes, until tops are golden brown.

Tips: Be careful not to overmix, or your corn bread will be dry and crumbly; this recipe is surprisingly moist. Serve with honey or all-fruit spread.

Nutritional Data for One Serving (1 Large Square): Calories: 254, Calories from Fat: 48, Total Fat: 5g, Saturated Fat: 0g, Cholesterol: 2mg, Sodium: 253mg, Total Carbohydrate: 42g, Dietary Fiber: 3g, Sugars: 2g, Protein: 9g, Vitamin A: 6%, Vitamin C: 2%, Calcium: 11%, Iron: 10%

Dill/Cottage Cheese Bread

Makes 2 loaves

Source: A neighbor downstairs at Canterbury Gardens Apartments gave me this recipe.

Combine in a small bowl:

½ **cup very warm water**
2 **packages (or 5 teaspoons) dry yeast**

Set aside. In a separate bowl, combine:

4 **tablespoons sugar (or 3 tablespoons honey)**
2 **tablespoons melted margarine**
1 **tablespoon dry minced onion**
2 **teaspoons dill weed**
2 **teaspoons salt**
½ **teaspoon baking soda**
4 **egg whites**

Combine two mixtures. Heat in a saucepan until lukewarm:

2   cups low-fat cottage cheese

Add cottage cheese to other ingredients. Slowly add, a little at a time:

3   cups white flour
2   cups whole wheat flour

Blend well. Cover. Let rise for 50 to 60 minutes in a warm place until doubled in size. Coat two loaf pans with nonstick cooking spray. Divide dough into two pans. Let rise for 30 to 40 minutes. Bake in a preheated 350 degree oven for 30 minutes, until golden brown.

Variations: The original recipe calls for 4 teaspoons dill weed in place of 2 teaspoons dill weed; I like this milder version better.
Tips: This is a moist, hearty bread: really tasty!

Nutritional Data for One Serving (1 Slice): Calories: 157, Calories from Fat: 18, Total Fat: 2g, Saturated Fat: 1g, Cholesterol: 2mg, Sodium: 349mg, Total Carbohydrate: 27g, Dietary Fiber: 2g, Sugars: 3g, Protein: 8g, Vitamin A: 2%, Vitamin C: 0%, Calcium: 3%, Iron: 8%

French Bread

Makes 4 loaves

Source: My sister-in-law, Joan Alden, gave me this recipe.

In a small bowl, dissolve:

2   packages (or 5 teaspoons) dry yeast
1   cup very warm water

In a larger bowl, combine:

2   cups very warm water
2   tablespoons sugar (or 1½ tablespoons honey)
2   tablespoons olive or canola oil
3   teaspoons salt

Add second mixture to the first and mix well. Gradually stir in:

5   cups white flour
3   cups whole wheat flour

Work through dough with a large spoon until blended. Add extra flour if needed. Let set for 10 minutes. Stir again thoroughly with spoon. Repeat the stirring process every 10 minutes for three more times, a total of five times in one hour. Turn dough onto floured surface and divide into four pieces. Shape into balls and let rise for 10 minutes. Roll out flat, then roll up firmly. Place on cookie sheets. Score diagonally five times on each top. Let rise until doubled. Bake in a preheated 400 degree oven for 30 to 35 minutes.

Variations: Use four cups *each* of whole wheat and white flour for a lighter bread.

Tips: Lightly coat the bread tops with butter-flavor cooking spray during the last 10 minutes of baking for a golden crust. Freeze extra loaves.

Nutritional Data for One Serving (1 Slice): Calories: 98, Calories from Fat: 9, Total Fat: 1g, Saturated Fat: 0g, Cholesterol: 0mg, Sodium: 161mg, Total Carbohydrate: 19g, Dietary Fiber: 2g, Sugars: 1g, Protein: 3g, Vitamin A: 0%, Vitamin C: 0%, Calcium: 1%, Iron: 6%

French Toast

Serves 6

Source: Adapted from a recipe in *The $30 a Week Grocery Budget, Volume I,* by Donna McKenna.

Combine in a small bowl:

1⅓ cups skim milk
4 egg whites

Beat together until foamy. Pour into a shallow wide bowl, big enough for a slice of bread to lie flat. Set aside. Preheat a large, nonstick frying pan until hot. Coat with nonstick cooking spray. Dip each side of:

12 pieces of bread

in the egg wash very quickly (don't let it soak) and immediately place in the hot pan. Turn once, when underside is golden brown. Remove from pan when the other side browns. Add more nonstick cooking spray and dipped bread slices until all the liquid is used.

Variations: Top with cinnamon and/or sugar, molasses, or honey. Or try this fancy brunch recipe: Spread fat-free cream cheese or strawberry preserves between two slices bread. Dip top and bottom in egg wash (above) and sprinkle lightly with cinnamon. "Fry" in nonstick pan as usual. Cover a few minutes so heat penetrates middle filling.

Tips: Keep your pan well coated with cooking spray, as the bread slices stick easily.

Nutritional Data for One Serving (2 Slices): Calories: 165, Calories from Fat: 18, Total Fat: 2g, Saturated Fat: 0g, Cholesterol: 1mg, Sodium: 335mg, Total Carbohydrate: 28g, Dietary Fiber: 0g, Sugars: 2g, Protein: 8g, Vitamin A: 3%, Vitamin C: 1%, Calcium: 12%, Iron: 9%

Granola

Serves 4

Source: Adapted from—and greatly modified from—a more complicated recipe in *The Enchanted Broccoli Forest: and Other Timeless Delicacies.**

In a large, heavy skillet (preferably cast iron), pour:

3 cups uncooked rolled oats

Turn on heat to medium low and stir constantly for 15 minutes. Sprinkle in:

¼ cup (packed) brown sugar
¼ teaspoon salt

Cook for a few more minutes, still stirring. Remove from heat. Serve hot or cold.

Variations: Add wheat germ, sesame seeds, nuts, coconut, raisins, etc. to your granola. (I kept mine simple, low-fat, and cheap!)

Tips: This granola is so good it's *worth* the long stirring time. (Read a book while you stand at the stove!) I like it better than the heavy-syrup version.

*This recipe is changed so much that I consider it my own. Still, I wanted readers to be aware of the original, excellent cookbook that was its source.

Nutritional Data for One Serving (¾ Cup): Calories: 285, Calories from Fat: 34, Total Fat: 4g, Saturated Fat: 1g, Cholesterol: 0mg, Sodium: 141mg, Total Carbohydrates: 54g, Dietary Fiber: 6g, Sugars: 1g, Protein: 10g, Vitamin A: 1%, Vitamin C: 0%, Calcium: 4%, Iron: 16%

Healthy Bran Muffins

Serves 8

Source: Adapted from a recipe by Jan Kent, author of
A Taste of Dutch cookbook.

Preheat oven to 400 degrees. Mix together in a large bowl:

2 **cups whole wheat flour**
1 **cup bran, flakes or raw**
2 **tablespoons baking powder**
1 **teaspoon salt**

Set aside. Beat together in a separate bowl:

4 **egg whites**
2 **cups skim milk**
½ **cup molasses**
½ **cup applesauce**

Add dry ingredients to eggs/milk mixture, and stir just well enough to moisten flour. Coat muffin tins with nonstick cooking spray. Fill ⅔ full. Bake for about 15 minutes, until nicely browned.

Variations: Add raisins or diced dates to the batter. Once, when I made this recipe, I was out of bran and substituted one cup of bran cereal (it worked). Add more molasses for sweeter muffins.

Tips: I usually double or triple this recipe and freeze the extras for breakfasts.

Nutritional Data for One Serving (2 Muffins): Calories: 205, Calories from Fat: 8, Total Fat: 1g, Saturated Fat: 0g, Cholesterol: 1mg, Sodium: 396mg, Total Carbohydrate: 43g, Dietary Fiber: 5g, Sugars: 4g, Protein: 9g, Vitamin A: 4%, Vitamin C: 3%, Calcium: 26%, Iron: 29%

Nut Raisin Bread

Makes two loaves

Source: A 20-year-old magazine article!

Preheat oven to 325 degrees. Combine in a medium-size saucepan:

2   cups raisins
1   cup water

Bring to a boil; turn off heat, and cool. Combine in a large bowl:

4   cups whole wheat flour
1   tablespoon baking soda
1   teaspoon salt

Set aside. In another large bowl, combine:

2   cups honey
8   egg whites
¼   cup olive or canola oil
2   teaspoons vanilla

Beat until well-blended. Set aside. Drain water from raisins. Add raisins, plus the following to honey mixture:

2   cups mashed bananas
1   cup pecans or walnuts, chopped

Add flour mixture, stirring just to blend all ingredients. Do not over-mix. Spray two loaf pans with nonstick cooking spray. Divide batter between two pans coated lightly with nonstick cooking spray. Bake for one hour. Lower oven temperature to 250 degrees and continue to bake for an additional 30 minutes, or until a wooden toothpick inserted in center comes out clean.

Variations: Omit nuts and/or reduce raisins, for cheaper, lower-fat bread.

Tips: The final bread is dark and dense, with a very "healthy" taste.

Nutritional Data for One Serving (1 Slice): Calories: 310, Calories from Fat: 64, Total Fat: 7g, Saturated Fat: 1g, Cholesterol: 0mg, Sodium: 290mg, Total Carbohydrate: 63g, Dietary Fiber: 4g, Sugars: 14g, Protein: 5g, Vitamin A: 0%, Vitamin C: 5%, Calcium: 2%, Iron: 9%

Oatmeal Pancakes

Serves 4 to 6

Source: Me!

Combine in a large bowl:

2   cups whole wheat flour
½   cup brown sugar
4   teaspoons baking powder
½   teaspoon salt

Set aside. In another bowl, beat together:

4   egg whites
1   cup cooked oatmeal
2   cups skim milk
¼   cup canola or olive oil
¼   cup applesauce

Combine the two mixtures and blend until smooth. For each pancake, pour ¼ cup batter onto a hot, nonstick skillet. Cook until bubbles begin to form on top, turn and brown other side.

Variations: This recipe is *very* flexible! Make the batter thicker or thinner, as you prefer. For a treat, add chocolate chips, nuts, or bits of banana. Omit cooked oatmeal, or replace it with ¾ cup dry oats soaked in ½ cup hot water.

Tips: These pancakes are so moist you don't need syrup. I usually serve them with a dusting of powdered sugar on top. But if you prefer, make the easy, rich, low-fat syrup recipe below.

Nutritional Data for One Serving (5 or 6 3″ Pancakes): Calories: 429, Calories from Fat: 112, Total Fat: 12g, Saturated Fat: 1g, Cholesterol: 2mg, Sodium: 332mg, Total Carbohydrate: 69g, Dietary Fiber: 7g, Sugars: 5g, Protein: 14g, Vitamin A: 6%, Vitamin C: 4%, Calcium: 19%, Iron: 15%

Pancake Syrup

Combine in a saucepan:

3   cups brown sugar
1½   cups water

Bring to a boil and stir occasionally, until sugar dissolves. Remove from heat. Stir in:

1   teaspoon vanilla

Serve hot or cold.

Popovers

Makes 12 popovers

Source: Adapted from a recipe in *The $30 a Week Grocery Budget,*
Volume I, by Donna McKenna.

Preheat oven to 450 degrees. Combine in a large bowl:

1   cup whole wheat flour
1   cup white flour
3   tablespoons sugar (or 2 tablespoons honey)
4   egg whites
2   cups skim milk

Coat a 12-count muffin tin with nonstick cooking spray. Fill ⅓ full with popover batter. Bake at 450 degrees for 10 minutes, then reduce heat to 350 degrees and bake for an additional 15 to 20 minutes.

Variations: Popovers can be served as is, with all-fruit jam, or stuffed with nearly anything imaginable: diced meats, vegetables, cheeses, fruit mixtures, puddings, etc. We enjoy them plain, but these moist, delicious rolls could be the base for a main dish.

Tips: I like this recipe because it's fast, easy, and good. Do not open the oven until after 30 minutes of baking or the popovers may fall. It's a little tricky to get them to "puff." It may take you a few tries before you're able to make this work, but even flattened popovers taste wonderful. Do not use paper baking cups: the popovers really *stick!*

Nutritional Data for One Serving (2 Popovers): Calories: 141, Calories from Fat: 6, Total Fat: 1g, Saturated Fat: 0g, Cholesterol: 1mg, Sodium: 80mg, Total Carbohydrate: 27g, Dietary Fiber: 3g, Sugars: 12g, Protein: 8g, Vitamin A: 5%, Vitamin C: 1%, Calcium: 11%, Iron: 5%

Poppy Seed Muffins

Makes about 2 dozen muffins

Source: Adapted from a recipe by Laura Fister, master baker!

Preheat oven to 400 degrees. Mix together in a bowl:

1	**cup whole wheat flour**
1	**cup white flour**
3	**teaspoons poppy seeds**
½	**teaspoon salt**
¼	**teaspoon baking soda**

In a separate bowl, combine:

1½	**cups nonfat yogurt**
1	**cup sugar**
4	**egg whites**
1	**teaspoon vanilla**

Cream together thoroughly. Combine the two mixtures. Coat two 12-count muffin tins with nonstick cooking spray. Spoon batter into muffin tins, filling each cup about ⅔ full. Bake for 15 to 20 minutes.

Variations: Poppy seeds can be omitted. Use plain yogurt or any flavor you prefer.

Tips: Buy your poppy seeds in bulk from a co-op or health food store for a tremendous savings. Homemade yogurt will also save you money (see Recipe Index).

Nutritional Data for One Serving (1 Muffin): Calories: 110, Calories from Fat: 3, Total Fat: 0g, Saturated Fat: 0g, Cholesterol: 0mg, Sodium: 78mg, Total Carbohydrate: 20g, Dietary Fiber: 1g, Sugars: 9g, Protein: 3g, Vitamin A: 0%, Vitamin C: 0%, Calcium: 4%, Iron: 3%

Pretzels

Makes 12 large pretzels

Source: Adapted from a recipe in *Cheap Eating* by Pat Edwards.

Preheat oven to 350 degrees. Combine in a small bowl:

1	**package (or 2½ teaspoons) yeast**
1⅓	**cups warm water**

Stir until yeast is dissolved. Add:

3	**cups white flour**
1	**cup whole wheat flour**
1	**teaspoon salt**
½	**teaspoon sugar**

Knead, adding flour as necessary, to form an easy-to-handle dough. Coat large bowl with nonstick cooking spray. Place dough in bowl; let rise until doubled. Divide dough into 12 pieces. Roll pieces into 12 inch strings. Tie into knots. Brush with:

1   egg, beaten

Sprinkle on:

Coarse salt and/or onion flakes

Bake for 15 to 20 minutes, until golden brown.

Variations: Use all white flour instead of part white, part whole wheat.

Tips: Pat Edwards says her pretzels are ". . . a wonderful rainy-day activity to share with young children." I agree.

Nutritional Data for One Serving (1 Pretzel): Calories: 158, Calories from Fat: 9, Total Fat: 1g, Saturated Fat: 0g, Cholesterol: 18mg, Sodium: 1251mg, Total Carbohydrate: 32g, Dietary Fiber: 2g, Sugars: 0g, Protein: 5g, Vitamin A: 1%, Vitamin C: 0%, Calcium: 2%, Iron: 10%

Pumpkin/Zucchini Bread

Makes 2 loaves

Source: Adapted from a recipe of my good friend, Lyn Hoeft.

Preheat oven to 325 degrees. Coat two loaf pans with nonstick cooking spray, then flour. Cream together in a large bowl:

- 1½   **cups sugar**
- ¾   **cup applesauce**
- ¼   **cup canola or olive oil**

Gradually add:

- 6   **egg whites**
- 2   **teaspoons vanilla**

Beat well. Grate:

- 3   **cups pumpkin *or* zucchini**

Add to sugar and oil mixture and blend well. In a separate bowl, combine:

- 1½   **cups white flour**
- 1½   **cups whole wheat flour**
- 1   **teaspoon cinnamon**
- 1   **teaspoon salt**
- 1   **teaspoon baking powder**
- 1   **teaspoon baking soda**

Combine the two mixtures and blend well. Bake for one hour, or until toothpick inserted in the center comes out clean.

Variations: This recipe is an excellent way to use up garden vegetables; I have substituted squash, for example, with good results. Add nuts if you prefer. Substitute one cup extra pumpkin or zucchini in place of the applesauce and oil.

Tips: My children love this bread and often ask for seconds and thirds. It makes a good, nutritious snack and doesn't take long to make. I usually double the recipe and freeze two of the four loaves.

Nutritional Data for One Serving (1 Slice): Calories: 170, Calories from Fat: 29, Total Fat: 3g, Saturated Fat: 0g, Cholesterol: 0mg, Sodium: 190mg, Total Carbohydrate: 33g, Dietary Fiber: 3g, Sugars: 15g, Protein: 4g, Vitamin A: 81%, Vitamin C: 4%, Calcium: 2%, Iron: 7%

Wheat Thins

Makes about four dozen small crackers

Source: Adapted from a recipe in *The Penny Pincher* newsletter, September/October 1992.

Preheat oven to 350 degrees. Mix together in a large bowl:

1¾　**cups whole wheat flour**
1½　**cups white flour**

Set aside. Combine in a blender:

⅓　**cup canola or olive oil**
1　**cup water**
¾　**teaspoon salt**

Blend until oil and water mix. Add liquid to dry mixture. Knead just enough to combine ingredients, as little as possible, until dough is smooth. Roll out very thinly (no more than ⅛-inch thick) on an ungreased cookie sheet. Use a knife to mark the size of the crackers, being careful not to cut completely through dough. Prick each cracker three times with a fork. Bake for about 30 to 35 minutes, until crackers are light brown and crisp.

Variations: Use a variety of seasonings: poppy seeds, sesame seeds, onion powder or salt, etc. to flavor the dough.

Tips: At first my children didn't care for the taste of these crackers, but they really grow on you. For picky eaters, replace some of the whole wheat flour with white flour.

Nutritional Data for One Serving (1 Large Cracker): Calories: 42, Calories from Fat: 15, Total Fat: 2g, Saturated Fat: 0g, Cholesterol: 0mg, Sodium: 34mg, Total Carbohydrate: 6g, Dietary Fiber: 1g, Sugars: 0g, Protein: 1g, Vitamin A: 0%, Vitamin C: 0%, Calcium: 0%, Iron: 2%

Side Dishes

Alfalfa Sprouts

Makes one quarter jar full of sprouts

Source: Adapted from information in *Whole Foods for the Whole Family* and personal experience.

Pour into a wide-mouthed quart jar:

About ¼ cup alfalfa seeds
Enough tepid water to cover the seeds
(plus a little more)

Let sit for about 12 hours, or overnight. Cover lid of jar with cheese-cloth and secure with a heavy rubber band. Drain water into a bowl; reserve for watering houseplants (it has lots of vitamins and minerals!). Fill jar again with tepid water. Immediately turn jar upside down, at a 45-degree angle, in a sturdy bowl or pan, so that water can drain out. Cover jar loosely with a dark plastic bag. Place in a dark area like a cupboard or bread box. Twice a day, fill the jar with water, then drain out. In a few days, the sprouts will be fully grown and ready to eat.

Variations and Tips: Sprouts are incredibly easy to grow, and very healthy. Spread out your rinsing times as much as possible. Serve in salads, on sandwiches, or in stir-fries and stews for extra nutrition and virtually no extra calories. Buy your seeds from a health food store or a cooperative.

Nutritional Data for One Serving (1 Cup): Calories: 10, Calories from Fat: 2, Total Fat: 0g, Saturated Fat: 0g, Cholesterol: 0mg, Sodium: 2mg, Total Carbohydrate: 1g, Dietary Fiber: 1g, Sugars: 0g, Protein: 1g, Vitamin A: 1%, Vitamin C: 5%, Calcium: 1%, Iron: 2%

Basic Beans

Makes about 5 cups

Source: Various people and cookbooks.

Place in a large saucepan:

1   pound dried beans
1   teaspoon salt
About 8 cups water, enough to cover the beans

Soak overnight. In the morning, drain beans. Combine in the same large saucepan:

Soaked beans
1   teaspoon salt
8   more cups of water

Bring to a boil and boil for 10 minutes. Reduce heat. Cover and simmer 90 minutes or until beans are tender. Stir occasionally, adding more water if needed.

Variations and Tips: Cook presoaked beans in your Crock-Pot®, for two hours on high and 8 to 10 hours on low. Start with this recipe, then use it as a base for others like baked or refried beans.

Nutritional Data for One Serving (½ Cup): Calories from Fat: 5, Total Fat: 1g, Saturated Fat: 0g, Cholesterol: 0mg, Sodium: 413mg, Total Carbohydrate: 58g, Dietary Fiber: 7g, Sugars: 4g, Protein: 8g, Vitamin A: 4%, Vitamin C: 14%, Calcium: 6%, Iron: 17%

Broiled Eggplant, Etc.

Serves 4 to 6

Source: Experimentation!

Set oven temperature to broil. Mix together in a small, shallow bowl:

1 **egg white**
½ **cup skim milk**
½ **cup flour**
½ **teaspoon salt**
Dash of pepper

Stir until lump-free. Set aside. Coat broiler pan generously with non-stick cooking spray. Peel and slice thinly:

1 **small eggplant (or part of eggplant)**

Dip in batter; let excess drip off into batter bowl. Place dipped eggplant on broiler rack. Broil on one side until golden brown, about five minutes. Turn; broil until second side is browned, another five minutes.

Variations: Try this recipe with squash, tomatoes, or other similar garden vegetables.

Tips: I'm not much of an eggplant fan, but even I—and some of our children—like it served this way.

Nutritional Data for One Serving (About ½ Cup): Calories: 32, Calories from Fat: 2, Total Fat: 0g, Saturated Fat: 0g, Cholesterol: 0mg, Sodium: 198mg, Total Carbohydrate: 6g, Dietary Fiber: 0g, Sugars: 1g, Protein: 2g, Vitamin A: 2%, Vitamin C: 1%, Calcium: 3%, Iron: 1%

Coleslaw

Serves 6 to 8

Source: My mother.

Shred into narrow strips:

½ **medium cabbage**
1 **small onion**

Mix well. Set aside. In a separate bowl, combine:

1 **cup reduced-calorie Miracle Whip®**
½ **cup nonfat yogurt**
3 **tablespoons sugar**
1 **teaspoon paprika**

Pour Miracle Whip® mixture over cabbage and onion. Mix thoroughly. Chill before serving.

Variations: If you prefer a more tart taste, add a little vinegar to the coleslaw.

Tips: Cabbage is usually cheap and always healthy, a good vegetable to serve often.

Nutritional Data for One Serving (About ½ Cup): Calories: 154, Calories from Fat: 84, Total Fat: 9g, Saturated Fat: 0g, Cholesterol: 12mg, Sodium: 245mg, Total Carbohydrate: 16g, Dietary Fiber: 2g, Sugars: 9g, Protein: 2g, Vitamin A: 3%, Vitamin C: 69%, Calcium: 7%, Iron: 2%

Easy Baked Beans

Makes about 4 cups

Source (for the Barbeque Sauce): A recipe in *Cheap Eating,*
by Pat Edwards.

Preheat oven to 350 degrees. Drain:

4   cups cooked beans (any kind)

Pour into large casserole dish. Mix together a barbeque sauce in a small bowl:

1   medium onion, finely diced
1   cup ketchup
1   cup grape jelly (or whatever jelly is on hand)

Pour onto beans. Add:

Other seasonings to taste

Cover. Bake for an hour, stirring occasionally and adding liquid as needed, until beans are bubbly.

French Fries

Serves 8

Source: Adapted from a newspaper recipe that claimed *its* source
as a heart association's recommendation.

Cut into narrow strips:

8   large Idaho potatoes, unpeeled

Soak strips in a large bowl of ice water for two hours. Preheat oven
to broil setting. Drain and pat potato strips dry. Lightly coat large
cookie sheet with nonstick cooking spray. Arrange strips on pan so
that sides do not touch. Lightly coat *strips* with cooking spray. Broil
until "fries" are browned on one side, about 5 minutes; quickly turn.
Brown on second side, about 5 minutes.

Variations: Instead of broiling, bake fries (turn once after 15
minutes) for 30 minutes at 475 degrees. Peel the potatoes before
broiling, if you prefer.

Tips: For some reason, we've occasionally had potatoes that are
not quite "done" after the recommended broiling time. You may
want to microwave the potato strips for a few minutes before broiling.

Nutritional Data for One Serving (About 1 Cup Each): Calories: 183, Calories
from Fat: 4, Total Fat: 0g, Saturated Fat: 0g, Cholesterol: 0mg, Sodium:
17mg, Total Carbohydrate: 41g, Dietary Fiber: 4g, Sugars: 0g, Protein: 5g,
Vitamin A: 0%, Vitamin C: 69%, Calcium: 3%, Iron: 19%

Fresh Green Beans and Onions

Serves 4 to 6

Source: Me.

Buy a "mess" of fresh green beans at the produce stand. Wash, snap off end pieces, and cut into bite-size pieces. Place in the Crock-pot®:

Prepared green beans
1 onion, thinly sliced and diced
Enough water to just cover the beans

Cook on high for several hours, until beans are tender.

Variations and Tips: The Crock-Pot® uses less energy than a stove, and it doesn't heat up your kitchen. But if you prefer, you can prepare these beans on a burner. Try the same simple recipe with other fresh vegetables. Save the liquid (if you don't serve it with the beans) in a "soup pot" in your freezer for future use.

Nutritional Data for One Serving (1 Cup): Calories: 54, Calories from Fat: 4, Total Fat: 0g, Saturated Fat: 0g, Cholesterol: 0mg, Sodium: 5mg, Total Carbohydrate: 12g, Dietary Fiber: 3g, Sugars: 3g, Protein: 3g, Vitamin A: 8%, Vitamin C: 23%, Calcium: 6%, Iron: 9%

Frozen Fruit Delight

Serves 8 to 10

Source: Adapted from one of my mother's recipes.

Combine in a blender:

2 large, very ripe bananas, cut into pieces
½ can orange juice concentrate
1 small can crushed pineapple (in light syrup)
3 cups water

Whir until smooth. Pour thin layers into metal trays and freeze. Just before serving, slice into small pieces and thaw slightly.

Variations: The original recipe calls for four oranges with pulp (instead of orange juice), lemon juice and 1½ cups of sugar. My variation is cheaper and more nutritious.

Tips: I freeze bananas—simply tossing them as is into the freezer—when they reach a very ripe stage. Later, thaw the bananas slightly for a few seconds in the microwave, partially peel, then *squirt* into the blender! We often make Frozen Fruit Delight into popsicles.

Nutritional Data for One Serving (About ⅔ Cup): Calories: 63, Calories from Fat: 2, Total Fat: 0g, Saturated Fat: 0g, Cholesterol: 0mg, Sodium: 4mg, Total Carbohydrate: 16g, Dietary Fiber: 1g, Sugars: 10g, Protein: 1g, Vitamin A: 1%, Vitamin C: 44%, Calcium: 1%, Iron: 2%

Fruit Salad

Serves as many as you like!

Source: Sally Davis, longtime friend.

Combine in a large glass bowl:

Canned peach slices (packed in its own juice)
White grapes
Fresh strawberries, diced
Bananas, sliced
Blueberries, when in season

Variations: Limitless!
Tips: Use *whatever* fruit is in season and save money.

Nutritional Data: Too hard to figure, but with very few calories and no fat, this salad is healthy!

Golden Broccoli Salad

Serves 6

Source: *Healthy Exchanges Food Newsletter.**

3¼	cups chopped broccoli
1	cup shredded carrots
¼	cup chopped onion
¾	cup shredded Kraft reduced-fat Cheddar cheese (3 ounces)
2	tablespoons Hormel Bacon Bits
¾	cup Kraft fat-free mayonnaise
	Sugar substitute to equal 2 tablespoons sugar
1½	teaspoons prepared mustard
2	tablespoons skim milk

In a large bowl, combine broccoli, carrots, onion, Cheddar cheese and Bacon Bits. In a small bowl, combine mayonnaise, sugar substitute, mustard and skim milk. Add mixture to broccoli mixture. Toss gently to combine. Cover and refrigerate until ready to serve.

Serves 6 (¾ cup)
Each serving equals:
HE: 1½ Vegetable, ⅔ Protein, ¼ Slider, 12 Optional Calories
99 Calories, 3 gm Fat, 7 gm Protein, 11 gm Carbohydrate, 404 mg Sodium, 2 gm Fiber
Diabetic: 2 Vegetable, ½ Meat

*Note: The format of this recipe differs from most others in this book at JoAnna Lund's—the author's—request that her original recipe remain exactly as it appeared in her newsletter.

Greek Feta Salad

Serves 4

Source: *Healthy Exchanges Food Newsletter.**

3	cups shredded lettuce
1¼	cups chopped cucumber
1	cup chopped tomato
½	cup chopped green bell pepper
¼	cup chopped onion
¾	cup cubed Feta cheese (3 ounces)
¼	cup sliced ripe olives (1 ounce)
2	tablespoons chopped fresh parsley *or* 2 teaspoons dried parsley flakes
¼	cup Kraft fat-free Ranch dressing
2	tablespoons Kraft fat-free Italian dressing

In a large bowl, combine lettuce, cucumber, tomato, green pepper, onion, Feta cheese, olives and parsley. Mix well. Cover and refrigerate. Just before serving, combine Ranch dressing and Italian dressing. Pour mixture over lettuce mixture. Toss gently to combine.

Serves 4 (2 cups)
Each serving equals:
HE: 3 Vegetable, 1 Protein, ¼ Fat, ¼ Slider, 7 Optional Calories
114 Calories, 5 gm Fat, 4 gm Protein, 13 gm Carbohydrate, 516 mg Sodium, 2 gm Fiber
Diabetic: 2 Vegetable, 1 Meat

HINT: If you can't find Feta cheese, use either reduced-fat Swiss cheese or any other cheese of your choice.

*Note: The format of this recipe differs from most others in this book at JoAnna Lund's—the author's—request that her original recipe remain exactly as it appeared in her newsletter.

Hashbrowns

Serves 6 to 8

Source: I've forgotten!

Cook in the microwave until slightly done but still firm:

6 large potatoes, peeled

Grate potatoes into a large bowl, and add:

1 large onion, grated

Heat a large, nonstick frying pan on the stove to medium hot. Mix potatoes and onions thoroughly and place grated potatoes and onions in hot pan. Cover. Cook for about 15 minutes, until underside is crispy and brown. Turn. Cook another 10 minutes. Add salt and pepper as desired.

Variations: Grate zucchini, squash, carrots, and/or bits of leftover vegetables into hashbrowns. Add diced chicken, and this side dish becomes an entree.

Tips: For a buttery taste, lightly coat potatoes (as they cook) with butter-flavored cooking spray.

Nutritional Data for One Serving (About ⅔ Cup): Calories: 148, Calories from Fat: 3, Total Fat: 0g, Saturated Fat: 0g, Cholesterol: 0mg, Sodium: 10mg, Total Carbohydrate: 34g, Dietary Fiber: 3g, Sugars: 1g, Protein: 3g, Vitamin A: 4%, Vitamin C: 37%, Calcium: 1%, Iron: 3%

Lemon Gelatin Delight

Serves 8 to 10

Source: The Ray family, from Quincy, Illinois, shared this recipe
when I visited their home one summer of my childhood.

Combine in a bowl:

2 small packages lemon gelatin
4 cups boiling water

Stir until dissolved. Pour into a 9 X 13 inch glass cake pan. Cool until
somewhat thickened. Fold in:

1 15-ounce can crushed pineapple (in light syrup),
   drained (reserve juice)
4 thinly sliced bananas

Chill until firm. Make topping by combining in a saucepan:

1 cup reserved pineapple juice
2 tablespoons flour
¼ cup sugar

Heat slowly, stirring constantly until smooth and thickened. Cool.
Add:

1 cup nonfat whipped topping

Spread entire mixture over gelatin. Chill for an hour or more before
serving.

Variations: Any flavor of gelatin works well, including sugar-
free. Add leftover fruit, or stir in juice instead of water.

Tips: Top with ½ cup low-fat cheddar cheese, if desired.

Nutritional Data for One Serving (1 Large Square): Calories: 178, Calories
from Fat: 3, Total Fat: 0g, Saturated Fat: 0g, Cholesterol: 0mg, Sodium:
58mg, Total Carbohydrate: 44g, Dietary Fiber: 1g, Sugars: 37g, Protein: 3g,
Vitamin A: 1%, Vitamin C: 15%, Calcium: 2%, Iron: 2%

Maple Waldorf Fruit Salad

Serves 8

Source: *Healthy Exchanges Food Newsletter.**

2   **cups cored and diced unpeeled apples (4 small)**
1   **cup diced bananas (1 medium)**
¼   **cup raisins**
1   **cup chopped celery**
½   **cup Kraft fat-free mayonnaise**
¼   **cup Cary's reduced-calorie maple syrup**
¼   **cup Peter Pan reduced-fat peanut butter**

In a medium bowl, combine apples, bananas, raisins and celery. In a small bowl, combine mayonnaise, maple syrup and peanut butter. Mix well until smooth. Add mayonnaise mixture to apple mixture. Toss gently to combine. Cover and refrigerate until ready to serve.

Serves 8 (½ cup)
Each serving equals:
HE: 1 Fruit, ¼ Fat, ¼ Protein, 15 Optional Calories
118 Calories, 3 gm Fat, 2 gm Protein, 21 gm Carbohydrate, 164 mg Sodium, 2 gm Fiber
Diabetic: 1 Fruit, ½ Fat

HINT: To plump up raisins without "cooking," place in a glass measuring cup and microwave on HIGH for 20 seconds.

*Note: The format of this recipe differs from most others in this book at JoAnna Lund's—the author's—request that her original recipe remain exactly as it appeared in her newsletter.

Mashed Potatoes

Serves 8 to 10

Source: Many sources, but with special thanks to JoAnn Knapp,
someone (at last) who helped me *master* this dish.

Boil in lightly salted water, just enough to cover:

8 medium Russet potatoes, peeled

When potatoes are tender and break easily with a fork, drain. Mash.
Beat in:

½ cup nonfat yogurt
¼ cup skim milk
¼ cup parsley, finely chopped
1 teaspoon onion powder
1 teaspoon salt
¼ teaspoon black pepper

Blend well, until potatoes are creamy. Serve with low-fat gravy (see
Recipe Index).

Variations: Spices are entirely up to you; I wrote down the combination I like.

Tips: Until this year, I've never had any luck making lump-free
mashed potatoes. My friend JoAnn tells me the secret is to boil the
potatoes just long enough that they flake easily, but not so long that
the cooking water clouds and potatoes are gluelike. Watch carefully
and check often, and your potatoes will be perfect.

Nutritional Data for One Serving (About ⅔ Cup): Calories: 114, Calories from
Fat: 2, Total Fat: 0g, Saturated Fat: 0g, Cholesterol: 0mg, Sodium: 257mg,
Total Carbohydrate: 26g, Dietary Fiber: 2g, Sugars: 3g, Protein: 3g, Vitamin
A: 1%, Vitamin C: 19%, Calcium: 5%, Iron: 3%

Pasta Salad

Serves 8 to 10

Source: Adapted from a recipe shared by my friend, JoAnn Knapp.

Following package directions, prepare:

1   12-ounce package colored spiral pasta

Drain and pour into a large bowl. Add:

3   cups fresh vegetables, chopped
1   green bell pepper, chopped
2   tablespoons fresh parsley, chopped

Pour on just enough:

Nonfat Italian salad dressing

to lightly moisten vegetables. Toss gently.

Variations: Choose any fresh veggies you like.
Tips: To make this dish healthier, use vegetable pasta.

Nutritional Data for One Serving (About ½ Cup): Calories: 169, Calories from Fat: 5, Total Fat: 1g, Saturated Fat: 0g, Cholesterol: 0mg, Sodium: 217mg, Total Carbohydrate: 35g, Dietary Fiber: 3g, Sugars: 3g, Protein: 6g, Vitamin A: 72%, Vitamin C: 66%, Calcium: 3%, Iron: 13%

Potato Chowder

Serves 8 to 10 "who are very, very hungry," says Jan

Source: Adapted from a recipe in *A Taste of Dutch* cookbook
by Jan Kent.

In a large Dutch oven or kettle, combine:

4   cups peeled, diced potatoes
1   cup grated carrot
½   cup finely chopped onion

1 **tablespoon parsley flakes**
1 **teaspoon salt**
¼ **teaspoon pepper**
4 **chicken bouillon cubes (or equivalent broth powder)**

Cover with water one inch above vegetables. Cook until tender, about 15 to 20 minutes. Do not drain. In a separate pan, scald:

6 **cups skim milk**

Heat until tiny bubbles form around the edge of the pan. Remove 1½ cups milk and add:

2 **tablespoons butter**
½ **cup flour**

to 1½ cups hot milk. Stir with a wire whisk until smooth. Add remaining hot milk to undrained vegetables, then stir in thickened milk. Blend well. Simmer for 15 minutes on low heat.

Variations: Add bits of leftover veggies and meat. Use reduced-fat or nonfat margarine.

Tips: Jan suggests serving this chowder with whole wheat bread. "What a treat!" she says. The Barfields think so, too.

Nutritional Data for One Serving (A *Big* Bowl): Calories: 202, Calories from Fat: 28, Total Fat: 3g, Saturated Fat: 2g, Cholesterol: 10mg, Sodium: 871mg, Total Carbohydrate: 35g, Dietary Fiber: 3g, Sugars: 8g, Protein: 9g, Vitamin A: 47%, Vitamin C: 39%, Calcium: 22%, Iron: 8%

Refried Beans

Makes about 4 cups

Drain:

4 **cups cooked Basic Beans**

Reserve:

1 **cup liquid**

In a large nonstick skillet, heat beans and liquid over medium heat. Mash beans until smooth. Continue cooking, stirring constantly, about five minutes, or until beans thicken.

Nutritional Data for One Serving (½ Cup): Calories: 118, Calories from Fat: 5, Total Fat: 1g, Saturated Fat: 0g, Cholesterol: 0mg, Sodium: 413mg, Total Carbohydrate: 58g, Dietary Fiber: 7g, Sugars: 4g, Protein: 8g, Vitamin A: 4%, Vitamin C: 14%, Calcium: 6%, Iron: 17%

Scalloped Potatoes

Serves 6

Source: Adapted from a recipe in *Cheap Eating* by Pat Edwards.

Preheat oven to 325 degrees. Coat a three-quart casserole dish with nonfat cooking spray; set aside. Thinly slice:

4   cups peeled, sliced potatoes
1   large onion

Place one-third of the potatoes and onions in the casserole dish. Dot with:

1   teaspoon reduced-calorie margarine

Repeat with two more layers, and

2   (more) teaspoons reduced calorie margarine

with one teaspoon for each layer. Set aside. In a quart jar, place:

6   tablespoons flour
½   cup dry milk
1   teaspoon salt
¼   teaspoon pepper

Seal and shake thoroughly. Add to jar:

3   cups skim milk

Reseal and shake until all flour is dissolved. Pour milk mixture over potato mixture. Add enough milk to cover potatoes, if needed. Bake for 1½ hours, until potatoes break easily with a fork.

Variations and Tips: For **Potato-Lentil Casserole,** substitute one cup lentils for half of the potatoes and increase the milk to 3½ cups.

For **Au Gratin Potatoes,** add 1½ to 2 cups cubed cheese (choose a lower-fat variety) to the scalloped potatoes recipe.

Nutritional Data for One Serving of Scalloped Potatoes (About ⅔ Cup): Calories: 238, Calories from Fat: 15, Total Fat: 2g, Saturated Fat: 0g, Cholesterol: 3mg, Sodium: 482mg, Total Carbohydrate: 46g, Dietary Fiber: 3g, Sugars: 6g, Protein: 11g, Vitamin A: 14%, Vitamin C: 56%, Calcium: 24%, Iron: 9%

Stuffed Potatoes

Serves as many as needed

Source: My friend, Sally Davis, worked at a restaurant that served
these delicious potatoes.

Scrub potatoes with a brush and water until clean. Cook, either in the oven or microwave, until potato feels soft when pressed between two fingers covered with a hot pad. Cooking time in the oven is about 40 to 60 minutes at 425 degrees, or 60 to 80 minutes at 375 degrees (if you're already baking something else at that temperature). Microwave time varies significantly: plan on 10 to 15 minutes.

Top potatoes with one of the following combinations:

Chili (see Recipe Index) and reduced-fat, grated cheese
Taco meat, shredded lettuce, diced tomatoes, black olives,
 grated reduced-fat cheese, low-fat sour cream
Steamed broccoli spears and reduced-fat Cheddar
Zucchini slices, diced tomatoes, diced onions, basil, salt and
 pepper, part-skim mozzarella cheese
Pizza sauce, Italian seasonings, part-skim mozzarella cheese
Cooked, diced ham and shredded cheese

Variations and Tips: Make up your own! My mother's variation of this recipe is **Twice-Baked Potatoes:** Cook potatoes as above. Cool. Hollow out potato skins and make mashed potatoes. Refill skins with mashed potatoes. Top with low-fat cheese. Bake or microwave until potatoes are reheated.

Nutritional Data: Too hard to figure, with all these options!

Stuffing

Serves 8

Source: Adapted from a recipe in *Cheap Eating* by Pat Edwards.

Combine in a one-quart saucepan:

1   tablespoon reduced-fat margarine, melted
1   onion, finely chopped

Add:

2   teaspoons sage
2   cloves garlic (or 2 teaspoons garlic powder)

Mix well. Lightly toss in:

8   cups dried bread cubes

Add:

4   cups defatted chicken broth *or* prepared bouillon

Bread may seem to melt but should hold its form. Use to stuff a turkey or chicken, or bake in a casserole dish coated with nonstick cooking spray for 35 to 40 minutes at 350 degrees.

Variations: Add ½ to 1 cup chopped celery, 1½ cups sliced mushrooms, 1 cup cooked poultry, or ½ cup raisins to stuffing.

Tips: Make your own bread cubes, from leftover bread ends and pieces you've collected in your freezer, rather than buying the pre-packaged kind.

Nutritional Data for One Serving (1 Cup): Calories: 116, Calories from Fat: 24, Total Fat: 3g, Saturated Fat: 1g, Cholesterol: 1mg, Sodium: 559mg, Total Carbohydrate: 17g, Dietary Fiber: 1g, Sugars: 2g, Protein: 5g, Vitamin A: 2%, Vitamin C: 2%, Calcium: 5%, Iron: 7%

Whole Wheat Pasta

Serves 6

Source: Adapted from a combination of recipes in cookbooks, memories of Mother's noodle-making, and my own experimenting.

Combine in a large bowl:

2 cups whole wheat flour
1 cup white flour
¾ cup water
2 egg whites, well-beaten
1 tablespoon canola or olive oil
½ teaspoon salt

Knead until dough forms a ball and feels smooth. Add a little more water if needed. Dough should be stiff but manageable. Lay out, covered, on a floured surface. Let rest for 10 minutes.

To make noodles, divide dough in half. Roll out one piece to about ¹⁄₁₆ inch thickness, turning often and adding flour as needed. Roll up lightly into a cylinder. Cut into strips, whatever size you like (about ⅛ to ¼ inch for noodles, for example). Unroll noodles; place on a cookie sheet to dry. Repeat the process with the second half of the dough. To cook pasta, in a large saucepan, bring to a boil:

8 cups water
1 teaspoon salt

Add pasta. Cook from five to 10 minutes, until pasta is tender. Drain.

Variations: Use a food processor or heavy-duty mixer to prepare the dough.

Tips: This pasta takes time, but the taste and nutrition is worth it!

Nutritional Data for One Serving (About ⅔ Cup Cooked Noodles): Calories: 244, Calories from Fat: 30, Total Fat: 3g, Saturated Fat: 0g, Cholesterol: 0mg, Sodium: 199mg, Total Carbohydrate: 46g, Dietary Fiber: 6g, Sugars: 1g, Protein: 9g, Vitamin A: 0%, Vitamin C: 0%, Calcium: 2%, Iron: 13%

Miscellaneous Recipes

Dragon Sauce

Makes a little more than 3 cups

Source: Adapted from a recipe in *Dinner's in the Freezer*
by Jill Bond.

In a saucepan, evenly mix:

3   cups peach nectar
3   tablespoons cornstarch

Make sure lumps are all gone. Add:

¼   cup fructose (or ½ cup sugar)
¼   cup vinegar
1 to 2   tablespoons soy sauce

Cook over medium heat until thick and transparent, about 10 minutes.

Variations **and Tips:** Jill says, "I like to buy the #10 can of peaches, make a cobbler with the peaches, and use the syrup for this sauce. To make it extra rich, save out some of the peaches, blend them until they're semiliquid with small peach pieces visible. Add these pureed peaches to the sauce. This goes well with egg rolls, over chicken and duckling. It's even delicious over rice." Use more cornstarch for a thicker sauce, less for a thinner one. Substitute pineapple, apricot, and/or plum juice/syrup for peach nectar.

Nutritional Data for One Serving (¼ Cup): Calories: 75, Calories from Fat: 0, Total Fat: 0g, Saturated Fat: 0g, Cholesterol: 0mg, Sodium: 133mg, Total Carbohydrate: 19g, Dietary Fiber: 0g, Sugars: 8g, Protein: 0g, Vitamin A: 2%, Vitamin C: 5%, Calcium: 0%, Iron: 1%

Drinks

Here are some quick, easy ideas for drinks. For more suggestions, see Chapter Three: Other Ways To Beat the System, under "Make Or Cook Your Own."

Diet Hot Chocolate

> Source: A recipe from our first year of marriage!

Mix together in a large cup:

½   cup dry milk powder
1   teaspoon cocoa
      Sweetener equivalent to 2 teaspoons sugar
      Enough boiling (or very *hot*) water to fill cup

Mix thoroughly. Top with marshmallows, if desired.

Abbreviated Nutritional Data (Per Cup): 129 Calories, 0 Fat, 19g Carbohydrate, 0 Sugar, 13g Protein.

Florida Cracker Lemonade

> Source: A recipe in *Dinner's In The Freezer* by Jill Bond.

Place several lemons in very hot water for 10 minutes, or microwave for 30 seconds. Juice. Heat the liquid in a small saucepan, adding 1 teaspoon fructose (or 2 teaspoons sugar) per lemon juiced. Stir until dissolved. In a pitcher, add juice mixture to 2 cups water per lemon used. Slice a lemon very thinly and float rings in the juice.

Abbreviated Nutritional Data (Per Glass): 27 Calories, 0 Fat, 10g Carbohydrate, 5g Sugars.

Smoothie

> Source: A combination of various recipes.

Combine in a blender: 1½ cups skim milk, 1 large diced banana, 1 tablespoon honey, 1 teaspoon vanilla. Blend until *smooth!*

Abbreviated Nutritional Data (2 Cup Serving, A Large Milkshake Glass): 313 Calories, 1g Fat, 63g Carbohydrate, 51g Sugars, 14g Protein.

Sun Tea

Fill a half-gallon glass jar with water. Add three teabags of your favorite brand of tea. Cover loosely. Set out in the sun. Brewed tea will be ready in a few hours.

Low-Fat French Salad Dressing

Makes about 3 cups

Source: Mom.

Combine in a blender:

¾ **cup sugar**
½ **cup vinegar**
½ **cup ketchup**
1 **teaspoon celery seeds**
1 **teaspoon paprika**
1 **teaspoon salt**
1 **teaspoon onion juice**

Mix together thoroughly.

Variations: Finely chopped onions can substitute for onion juice. I have also used other kinds of seeds, such as dill, instead of celery. You can try whatever spices you have on hand.

Tips: Store in the refrigerator in a tightly covered jar. Shake well before serving.

Nutritional Data for One Serving (2 Tablespoons): Calories: 31, Calories from Fat: 0, Total Fat: 0g, Saturated Fat: 0g, Cholesterol: 0mg, Sodium: 157mg, Total Carbohydrate: 8g, Dietary Fiber: 0g, Sugars: 7g, Protein: 0g, Vitamin A: 1%, Vitamin C: 2%, Calcium: 0%, Iron: 1%

Low-Fat Ranch Salad Dressing

Makes 2 cups

Source: Adapted from several combined recipes.

Combine in a blender:

1   **cup reduced-fat mayonnaise**
1   **cup buttermilk (see Milk Substitutes recipe)**
2   **tablespoons onion juice**
2   **teaspoons parsley, finely chopped**
¼   **teaspoon salt**
¼   **teaspoon garlic powder**
¼   **teaspoon paprika**
¼   **teaspoon black pepper**

Mix well. Store covered in the refrigerator.

Variations: Add more or less spice according to your taste. Substitute plain yogurt for mayonnaise. I sometimes use two tablespoons of onion powder in place of onion juice.

Tips: These two salad dressings are much cheaper than store-bought, nutritious *and* delicious!

Nutritional Data for One Serving (2 Tablespoons): Calories: 47, Calories from Fat: 37, Total Fat: 4g, Saturated Fat: 1g, Cholesterol: 6mg, Sodium: 65mg, Total Carbohydrate: 2g, Dietary Fiber: 0g, Sugars: 1g, Protein: 1g, Vitamin A: 1%, Vitamin C: 1%, Calcium: 2%, Iron: 0%

Milk Substitutes and Products*

Sweetened Condensed Milk

Mix in a blender until thickened:

1 cup dry nonfat milk powder
½ cup boiling water
⅔ cup sugar
3 tablespoons reduced-fat margarine, melted
Pinch of salt

Store in a tightly covered container in the refrigerator.

Tips: This recipe yields the same amount as one can of Eagle Brand milk and can be used in any recipe calling for it.

Nutritional Data for One Serving (1 Tablespoon): Calories: 13, Calories from Fat: 3, Total Fat: 0g, Saturated Fat: 0g, Cholesterol: 1mg, Sodium: 58mg, Total Carbohydrate: 1g, Dietary Fiber: 0g, Sugars: 1g, Protein: 2g, Vitamin A: 0%, Vitamin C: 1%, Calcium: 1%, Iron: 0%

Soured Milk or Buttermilk

Place in an empty one cup container:

1 tablespoon lemon juice

Fill to the top with:

Skim milk

Tips: Use in place of one cup buttermilk or one cup soured milk.

*I'm not sure of the sources for the first two Milk Substitutes and Products recipes, but Low-Fat Sour Cream is adapted from a recipe in *The New Lean Toward Health*. See Resources.

Low-Fat Sour Cream

Combine in a blender:

1   cup low-fat cottage cheese
1   tablespoon skim milk
2   tablespoons lemon juice

Blend until smooth.

Tips: You can also substitute one cup nonfat yogurt for one cup sour cream in many recipes.

Nutritional Data for One Serving (1 Tablespoon): Calories: 13, Calories from Fat: 3, Total Fat: 0g, Saturated Fat: 0g, Cholesterol: 1mg, Sodium: 58mg, Total Carbohydrate: 1g, Dietary Fiber: 0g, Sugars: 1g, Protein: 2g, Vitamin A: 0%, Vitamin C: 1%, Calcium: 1%, Iron: 0%

Whipped Topping

Makes about 2 cups

Source: A combination of several recipes, one from a newsletter, one from a book, and one from a magazine article, with my own adaptations.

Combine in a shallow, chilled bowl:

1   cup icy cold water
1   teaspoon lemon juice
1   package unflavored gelatin
Pinch of cream of tartar

With chilled beaters, blend in:

1   cup nonfat dry milk powder

Whip at high speed until light and fluffy, with soft peaks forming. Continue to beat, adding:

⅓   cup sugar
½   teaspoon vanilla

Serve at once, or chill.

Variations: Add a touch of cinnamon or a little more (or less) lemon juice, as you prefer.

Tips: You can cut down on the amount of time needed for whipping if you set the cold water in a metal bowl in the freezer, just until ice crystals start to form. The taste of this topping is delicious, though the consistency is more liquid than that of the store-bought version. You may need to beat the mixture for several minutes.

Nutritional Data for One Serving (2 Tablespoons): Calories: 33, Calories from Fat: 0, Total Fat: 0g, Saturated Fat: 0g, Cholesterol: 1mg, Sodium: 24mg, Total Carbohydrate: 6g, Dietary Fiber: 0g, Sugars: 4g, Protein: 2g, Vitamin A: 3%, Vitamin C: 1%, Calcium: 5%, Iron: 0%

Yogurt

Makes about 8 cups

Source: A combination of two recipes and personal experience.

Preheat oven to 200 degrees. Heat in a large saucepan:

2 quarts (8 cups) milk

Use candy thermometer to gauge when milk reaches 180 degrees. Remove from heat and cool to 112 degrees. Measure ¾ cup hot milk into a small pan. Stir into this smaller amount of milk:

4 to 6 tablespoons plain yogurt

one tablespoon at a time, mixing thoroughly each time. Pour ¾ cup milk and blended yogurt back into saucepan. Stir until well mixed. Reheat to 112 degrees if temperature has dropped. Pour into hot, sterilized jars; place yogurt-filled jars in a cake pan. Turn preheated oven **off.** Put cake pan into warm oven. Turn on oven light and leave jars in oven overnight. Yogurt will be ready in the morning.

Variations: Once yogurt is set, blend in any mixture of fruit, syrup, or juice you like.

Tips: If you have a yogurt maker, follow the manufacturer's directions and the above recipe. It's best to use whole or 2% milk rather than skim. New yogurt can be made from four to six tablespoons of *your* plain yogurt (providing the yogurt is no older than four to five days). Use yogurt in place of mayonnaise or sour cream in most recipes. You can even make your own "cream cheese," below.

Nutritional Data for One Serving (1 Cup): Calories: 130 Calories from Fat: 45, Total Fat: 5g, Saturated Fat: 3g, Cholesterol: 19mg, Sodium: 129mg, Total Carbohydrate: 12g, Dietary Fiber: 0g, Sugars: 12g, Protein: 9g, Vitamin A: 15%, Vitamin C: 4%, Calcium: 32%, Iron: 1%

Yogurt Cream Cheese

Stir plain unflavored yogurt and pour off liquid whey. Place a colander over a pan, and in the colander layer three large folds of cheesecloth. Empty yogurt onto cheesecloth layers so that liquid drains into pan below. Tie up ends of cheesecloth into a loose knot. Drain yogurt for eight hours (or overnight). Yogurt cheese should have the same consistency as cream cheese, but with a tangier taste.

Desserts

Apple Crisp

Serves 8 to 10

Source: Adapted from a recipe shared by Erma, cook at the day
care center where I once taught.

Preheat oven to 375 degrees. Peel and slice:

3 to 5 pounds apples

Coat a large cake pan with nonstick cooking spray. Place apple slices in pan and sprinkle with:

3 tablespoons sugar
2 teaspoons cinnamon

Set aside. In a medium-size bowl, combine:

1 cup whole wheat flour
1 cup brown sugar
½ cup rolled oats
⅓ cup melted low-fat or nonfat margarine

Mix well, until crumbly. Spoon over apples. Bake for 35 minutes, or until apples are tender and bubbly.

Variations: If apples are tart, sprinkle on more sugar. Substitute any seasonal fruit you like.

Tips: Serve hot or cold, plain, or with low-fat whipped topping.

Nutritional Data for One Serving (About ¾ Cup): Calories: 317, Calories from Fat: 41, Total Fat: 5g, Saturated Fat: 1g, Cholesterol: 0mg, Sodium: 87mg, Total Carbohydrate: 71g, Dietary Fiber: 5g, Sugars: 30g, Protein: 3g, Vitamin A: 9%, Vitamin C: 14%, Calcium: 4%, Iron: 8%

Applesauce Gingerbread

Serves 16

Source: From a recipe in *Secrets of Fat-Free Baking* by Sandra Woodruff.

Preheat oven to 325 degrees. Combine:

1½	cups unbleached flour
1	cup whole wheat flour
⅔	cup sugar
2½	teaspoons baking soda
1	teaspoon ground ginger
1	teaspoon ground cinnamon
1	teaspoon ground allspice

Stir to mix well. Add:

1½	cups unsweetened applesauce
1	cup molasses
3	egg whites

Stir to mix well. Coat a 9 X 13 inch pan with nonstick cooking spray. Spread the batter evenly in the pan, and bake at 325 degrees for 40 minutes, or just until a wooden toothpick inserted in the center of the cake comes out clean. Cool the cake for at least 20 minutes. Cut into squares and serve warm or at room temperature with a light whipped topping, if desired.

Variations (**my own idea**): Substitute three teaspoons apple pie spice for ginger, cinnamon *and* allspice.

Tips: The texture of low-fat cakes is different from that of "normal" cakes. Be prepared for more chewiness!

Nutritional Data for One Serving (1 Square): 157 calories, 0.3g fat, 3.1g protein, no cholesterol, 146mg sodium, 1.6g fiber, 38mg calcium, 255mg potassium, 1.7mg iron.

Baked Apples

Serves 6

Source: A recipe from my friend, JoAnn Knapp, among other sources.

Preheat oven to 400 degrees. Core, leaving ½ inch from the bottom intact:

6   medium apples

Measure out:

6   teaspoons raisins
6   teaspoons all-fruit spread, any flavor

Fill each cored apple with one teaspoon raisins, then one teaspoon spread. Coat baking dish with nonstick cooking spray. Place apples in baking dish. Cover with foil. Bake for 25 to 30 minutes, until apples are tender.

Variations: Fill the centers with all-fruit spread and a little maple syrup, omitting raisins. Or peel and cut up apples, spooning fruit spread and raisins over the top.

Nutritional Data for One Serving (1 Apple): Calories: 97, Calories from Fat: 6, Total Fat: 1g, Saturated Fat: 0g, Cholesterol: 0mg, Sodium: 6mg, Total Carbohydrate: 25g, Dietary Fiber: 3g, Sugars: 20g, Protein: 0g, Vitamin A: 1%, Vitamin C: 13%, Calcium: 1%, Iron: 2%

Baked Custard

Serves 8 to 10

Source: My dear mother's recipe files.

Preheat oven to 350 degrees. In a large saucepan, scald until nearly boiling:

4½   cups skim milk

Combine in a large bowl:

1   cup egg whites
¾   cup honey
½   teaspoon salt

Pour into scalded milk. Add:

1   teaspoon vanilla

Blend well. Pour custard into a large ovenproof casserole dish and place the dish in a baking pan filled with one inch of water. Set in oven. Bake for 50 to 60 minutes, or until knife inserted in center comes out clean.

Variations: Sprinkle with a little cinnamon just before baking. 2% milk makes a firmer custard; *don't* use reconstituted nonfat dry milk in this recipe.

Tips: This low-fat, nutritious dessert is truly delicious! Serve hot or well-chilled, as you like it.

Nutritional Data for One Serving (½ to ¾ Cup): Calories: 137, Calories from Fat: 2, Total Fat: 0g, Saturated Fat: 0g, Cholesterol: 2mg, Sodium: 207mg, Total Carbohydrate: 29g, Dietary Fiber: 0g, Sugars: 5g, Protein: 6g, Vitamin A: 7%, Vitamin C: 2%, Calcium: 15%, Iron: 1%

Bread Pudding

Serves 6

Source: A magazine article and my own adaptations.

Preheat oven to 350 degrees. Coat a 2-quart casserole dish with non-stick cooking spray. Combine in the casserole dish:

8   slices whole wheat bread, crusts trimmed, cubed
1   12-ounce can evaporated skim milk

Let stand for 10 minutes. Stir in:

½   cup raisins

Set aside. In a small bowl, beat together:

3   egg whites
1   whole egg
1   cup skim milk
½   cup brown sugar
1   teaspoon vanilla
½   teaspoon cinnamon

Pour over bread mixture. Bake for 45 to 50 minutes.

Variations: Leave out raisins. Serve hot with whipped topping.
Tips: Save the trimmed bread crusts and make them into croutons or bread sticks (see Recipe Index).

Nutritional Data for One Serving (About ¾ Cup): Calories: 281, Calories from Fat: 24, Total Fat: 3g, Saturated Fat: 1g, Cholesterol: 38mg, Sodium: 331mg, Total Carbohydrate: 54g, Dietary Fiber: 1g, Sugars: 10g, Protein: 12g, Vitamin A: 11%, Vitamin C: 17%, Calcium: 27%, Iron: 12%

Caramel Apricot Rice Pudding

Serves 6

Source: *Healthy Exchanges Food Newsletter.**

2 cups water
1 cup diced dried apricots (4½ ounces)
1⅓ cups dry instant Minute Rice (4 ounces)
1 (4 serving) pkg Jell-O sugar-free instant butterscotch
pudding mix
⅔ cup Carnation nonfat dry milk powder
1½ cups water
¼ cup Cool Whip Lite
1 teaspoon vanilla extract

In a medium saucepan, combine water and diced apricots. Bring mixture to a boil. Remove from heat. Stir in dry rice. Cover. Let set 15 minutes to cool. In a large bowl, combine dry pudding mix and dry milk powder. Add water. Mix well using a wire whisk. Blend in Cool Whip Lite and vanilla extract. Fold in cooled rice mixture. Mix gently to combine. Evenly spoon mixture into 6 dessert dishes. Refrigerate until ready to serve. Freezes well.

Serves 6
Each serving equals:
HE: 1 Fruit, ⅔ Bread, ⅓ Skim Milk, ¼ Slider, 2 Optional Calories
140 Calories, 0gm Fat, 4gm Protein, 31gm Carbohydrate, 264 mg Sodium, 2 gm Fiber
Diabetic: 1 Fat, ½ Starch, ½ Skim Milk

*Note: The format of this recipe differs from most others in this book at JoAnna Lund's—the author's—request that her original recipe remain exactly as it appeared in her newsletter.

Caramel Corn

Serves 24

Source: Adapted from a recipe shared by Erma Geiman,
family friend.

Preheat oven to 250 degrees. Prepare in a popcorn popper:

12   quarts (3 very large bowls, or 48 cups) air-popped corn

Set aside. Combine in a large, heavy-duty saucepan:

2   cups brown sugar
1½   sticks low-fat margarine
½   cup white syrup
¼   teaspoon cream of tartar
¼   teaspoon salt

Bring to a rolling boil. Let boil, stirring occasionally, for five minutes. Remove from heat. Add:

1½   teaspoon baking soda

Mix well. Working fast, stir hot caramel mixture into popped corn until thoroughly blended. Spread on cookie sheets coated with non-stick cooking spray. Bake for 30 minutes, stirring once or twice. Remove from oven. When lukewarm, break into small pieces. Cool completely. Store in airtight containers.

Variations: The original recipe makes a very rich candy, as the syrup is spread over 6 quarts of popped corn. (Sometimes I make a small batch like this for our neighbors!)

Tips: If the syrup cools before you are able to spread it all on the popcorn, reheat briefly on the stove. Caramel corn can be stored in the freezer for several months or in the refrigerator for a few weeks. This is one of my children's *favorite* treats.

Nutritional Data for One Serving (2 Cups): Calories: 193, Calories from Fat: 38, Total Fat: 4g, Saturated Fat: 1g, Cholesterol: 0mg, Sodium: 136mg, Total Carbohydrate: 39g, Dietary Fiber: 2g, Sugars: 5g, Protein: 3g, Vitamin A: 8%, Vitamin C: 0%, Calcium: 2%, Iron: 5%

Chocolate Tortilla Torte

Serves 6

Source: Adapted from a newspaper recipe. (I have no other
information except a little cutout rectangle!)

Pour into medium-size bowl:

1   cup skim milk
**1   (4-serving size) package chocolate sugar-free instant
    pudding mix**
¼ teaspoon cinnamon

Beat for two minutes with wire whisk. Gently stir in, until well-
blended:

½ cup whipped topping

Lay out:

5 (5 to 6 inch) flour tortillas

Spread about ¼ cup pudding mixture on one flour tortilla. Repeat
layers, ending with pudding mixture. Refrigerate, lightly covered, for
two to three hours. Garnish with a dollop of whipped topping.

Variations: I usually prepare this recipe the night *after* I've
served pudding for dessert, and saved back some leftover pudding.
Instead of pudding, combine whipped topping with all-fruit spread.

Tips: Garnish with chocolate syrup (cocoa and sugar mixed with
a little hot water).

Nutritional Data for One Serving (1 Generous Wedge): Calories: 128, Calories
from Fat: 19, Total Fat: 2g, Saturated Fat: 0g, Cholesterol: 1mg, Sodium:
170mg, Total Carbohydrate: 22g, Dietary Fiber: 0g, Sugars: 2g, Protein: 4g,
Vitamin A: 2%, Vitamin C: 1%, Calcium: 10%, Iron: 7%

Crystallized Grapes and Oranges

Serves 4

Source: Adapted from a recipe in *Cheap Eating* by Pat Edwards.

In a small bowl, lightly beat until foamy:

1 egg white

Roll in egg white:

3 cups seedless grapes
2 oranges or tangerines, cut in wedges

Immediately roll coated fruit in:

1 cup sugar

Let dry and serve.

Variations and Tips: Try a variety of grapes. Pat likes to serve this dessert for holidays.

Nutritional Data for One Serving (1¼ Cups)*: Calories: 273, Calories from Fat: 3, Total Fat: 0g, Saturated Fat: 0g, Cholesterol: 0mg, Sodium: 17mg, Total Carbohydrate: 70g, Dietary Fiber: 6g, Sugars: 70g, Protein: 2g, Vitamin A: 1%, Vitamin C: 99%, Calcium: 5%, Iron: 2%

*If you're surprised at how high in both sugar and calories this recipe is, it's because the nutritional analyst estimated ¼ cup sugar per serving (just as the recipe says). You can actually get by with much less sugar by *lightly* rolling the fruit in it, and cut both grams of sugar and calories considerably.

Five-Minute Chocolate Custard Pie

Serves 6 to 8

Source: I changed a recipe card to make this pie my own
low-fat creation.

Preheat oven to 350 degrees. Combine in a blender:

2   **cups skim milk**
8   **egg whites**
⅔   **cup sugar**
½   **cup flour**
⅓   **cup cocoa, sifted**
1   **teaspoon vanilla**
Pinch of salt

Set aside. Use:

1   **teaspoon low-fat margarine, melted**
2   **tablespoons flour**

to coat and flour two 8″ pie pans or ovenproof casserole dishes. Blend milk/egg mixture a few seconds, until smooth. Pour into pans or dishes. Bake for 30 minutes, or until knife inserted in center comes out clean.

Variations: Omit cocoa and add two teaspoons cinnamon.
Tips: This recipe actually takes me five minutes to assemble, and it even makes its own crust. We like the pie best when it's chilled for two hours or more before serving, but you can also serve it hot.

Nutritional Data for One Serving (1 Large Slice): Calories: 161, Calories from Fat: 5, Total Fat: 1g, Saturated Fat: 0g, Cholesterol: 1mg, Sodium: 151mg, Total Carbohydrate: 31g, Dietary Fiber: 0g, Sugars: 22g, Protein: 7g, Vitamin A: 7%, Vitamin C: 3%, Calcium: 9%, Iron: 3%

Fudge Brownies

Serves 36 (small squares)

Source: Adapted from "Very Best Fudge Brownies" in *Secrets of Fat-Free Baking* by Sandra Woodruff.

Preheat oven to 325 degrees. Melt:

4 (1-ounce) squares unsweetened baking chocolate

If using a microwave oven to melt chocolate, place the chocolate in a mixing bowl and microwave uncovered at high power for 3 to 4 minutes, or until almost melted. Remove the bowl from the microwave and stir in the chocolate until completely melted. If melting the chocolate on a stove top, place the chocolate in a small saucepan and cook over low heat, stirring constantly, until melted. Add to the chocolate:

1½ cups sugar
½ cup plus 1 tablespoon fat-free egg substitute
¾ cup prune butter (see note)
2 teaspoons vanilla

Stir to mix well. Stir in:

1 cup unbleached flour

Coat a 9 X 13 inch pan with nonstick cooking spray. Spread the batter evenly in the pan, and bake for 35 to 40 minutes or until edges are firm and the center is almost set. Cool to room temperature, cut into squares and serve.

Variations: When I tried this recipe, I used fresh pumpkin puree in place of prune butter; canned pumpkin works, too. Optional ingredients in this recipe include ¼ teaspoon salt and ¾ cup chopped walnuts.

Tips: If you're making a cutup party cake, this recipe works well, as the brownie mixture slices better than most cakes.

Nutritional Data Per Serving (1 Small Square, Without Optional Ingredients): Calories: 74, Fat: 1.7g, Protein: 1.3g, Cholesterol: 0mg, Sodium: 21mg, Fiber: 1.1g, Calcium: 6mg, Potassium: 72mg, Iron: 0.6mg

Prune Butter

To make prune butter, place 8 ounces pitted prunes (about 1⅓ cups) and 6 tablespoons water or fruit juice in a food processor. Process at high speed until the mixture is a smooth paste. (Mixture is too thick to be made in a blender.) Use immediately, or place in an airtight container and store for up to 3 weeks in the refrigerator. Yields one cup.

Gelatin Desserts

Sources: Magazine articles, cookbooks, friends' files, etc.

Here are some ideas for quick, healthy gelatin desserts.

Diet Gelatin

Serves 4

Mix together in a small saucepan:

½   **can of fruit-flavored diet soda**
1   **package plain gelatin**

Bring to a boil, stirring constantly. Mix well. Remove from heat. Add:

(Other) ½   **can of fruit-flavored diet soda**

Stir until completely dissolved. Chill until set.

Juice Gelatin

Follow the Diet Gelatin recipe, but substitute juice (orange, grape, apple, cherry; anything but pineapple) in place of diet soda.

Variations: Make a vegetable gelatin with grated carrots and finely diced celery. Add apples, raisins and nuts. Mash overly ripe bananas and blend into gelatin. Use up excess juice from canned fruits. This is the perfect place to "recycle" some carefully selected leftovers.

Tips: Make sure gelatin is completely dissolved in hot liquid before adding cold liquid.

Nutritional Data: Too many variables to tell!

Impossible Pumpkin Pie

Serves 6

Source: Adapted from a Bisquick® recipe card from long ago.

Preheat oven to 350 degrees. Coat a 9-inch pie pan with nonstick cooking spray and lightly flour. Combine in a blender:

1	**16-ounce can pumpkin**
1	**13-ounce can evaporated skim milk**
4	**egg whites**
¾	**cup sugar**
½	**cup Bisquick® baking mix**
2½	**teaspoons pumpkin pie spice**
2	**teaspoons vanilla**
1	**teaspoon melted butter**

Blend well, about one minute in blender, or two minutes with hand beater. Pour into pie pan. Bake about 50 to 55 minutes, until knife inserted in center comes out clean.

Variations: Instead of Bisquick®, substitute ½ cup flour, ½ teaspoon baking powder, and a pinch of salt.

Tips: This pie makes its own low-fat crust! Easy!

Nutritional Data for One Serving (1 Medium Wedge): Calories: 240, Calories from Fat: 22, Total Fat: 2g, Saturated Fat: 1g, Cholesterol: 4mg, Sodium: 244mg, Total Carbohydrate: 46g, Dietary Fiber: 2g, Sugars: 25g, Protein: 9g, Vitamin A: 175%, Vitamin C: 7%, Calcium: 23%, Iron: 8%

Oatmeal Crispies

Makes 4 dozen or more

Source: Mom's files!

Preheat oven to 350 degrees. Combine in a large bowl:

1   **cup sugar**
1   **cup brown sugar**
⅔   **cup applesauce**
⅓   **cup shortening**
4   **egg whites**

Stir in:

1   **cup whole wheat flour**
1   **cup white flour**
2   **cups rolled oats**
1   **teaspoon salt**
1   **teaspoon baking soda**

Mix well. Drop by tablespoonsful onto cookie sheets coated lightly with nonstick cooking spray. Bake for 8 to 10 minutes, or until very lightly browned.

Variations: Add tiny chocolate chips or raisins to the dough. Use more flour for a puffier kind of cookie; these are thin and crisp.

Tips: My favorite cookies are the ones with *mega*-fat: this recipe, for example, originally called for one cup shortening. I think these are the tastiest low-fat version I've tried.

Nutritional Data for One Serving (1 Cookie): Calories: 81, Calories from Fat: 15, Total Fat: 2g, Saturated Fat: 0g, Cholesterol: 0mg, Sodium: 77mg, Total Carbohydrate: 15g, Dietary Fiber: 1g, Sugars: 5g, Protein: 1g, Vitamin A: 0%, Vitamin C: 0%, Calcium: 1%, Iron: 2%

Orange Sherbet

Makes 1 ½ quarts (about 12 servings)

Source: Adapted from a recipe in *The Penny Pincher* newsletter,
April 1994.

Place in a small metal bowl, in the freezer:

1 can evaporated milk

Leave in freezer just until ice crystals begin to form, about 30 minutes.
Remove. Whip milk with an electric beater until stiff peaks form. Beat
in:

6 ounces frozen orange juice concentrate, thawed
⅓ cup sugar

Return to freezer and freeze until firm, about one to two hours.

Variations: Try other juices instead of orange juice.
Tips: This is a really delicious, cheap, healthy recipe: what more
could you ask for? I prefer to eat the sherbert when it's still the
consistency of whipped cream, before freezing solid.

Nutritional Data for One Serving (½ Cup): Calories: 69, Calories from Fat: 1,
Total Fat: 0g, Saturated Fat: 0g, Cholesterol: 1mg, Sodium: 37mg, Total Car-
bohydrate: 14g, Dietary Fiber: 0g, Sugars: 5g, Protein: 3g, Vitamin A: 4%,
Vitamin C: 37%, Calcium: 10%, Iron: 1%

Pineapple Torte

Serves 6

Source: *Healthy Exchanges Food Newsletter.**

1 cup canned crushed pineapple, packed in its own juice,
     drained, and reserve liquid (8 ounce can)
1 teaspoon lemon juice
1 (4 serving) pkg Jell-O sugar-free vanilla cook and serve
     pudding mix
⅔ cup Carnation nonfat dry milk powder
1 cup Cool Whip Lite
12 (2½") graham crackers, crushed (¾ cup)

Add enough water to reserved pineapple juice to make 1 cup liquid.
Pour liquid into medium saucepan. Add lemon juice, dry pudding
mix and dry milk powder. Mix well to combine. Cook over medium
heat until mixture thickens and starts to boil, stirring constantly. Remove from heat. Stir in pineapple. Cool 30 minutes. Fold in Cool
Whip Lite. Save 2 tablespoons graham cracker crumbs. Spread remaining crumbs in an 8X8-inch dish sprayed with butter-flavored
cooking spray. Pour pineapple mixture evenly over crumbs. Sprinkle
remaining crumbs evenly over top. Cover and freeze. About 15 minutes before serving, remove from freezer and let set. Cut into 6 pieces.

Serves 6
Each serving equals:
HE: ⅔ Bread, ⅓ Skim Milk, ⅓ Fruit, ¼ Slider, 15 Optional Calories
154 Calories, 3 gm Fat, 4 gm Protein, 28 gm Carbohydrate, 226 mg Sodium,
1 gm Fiber
Diabetic: 1 Starch, ½ Fruit, ½ Fat

HINT: Nilla crushed crumbs can be used instead of graham cracker crumbs.

*Note: The format of this recipe differs from most others in this book at JoAnna
Lund's—the author's—request that her original recipe remain exactly as it appeared in her newsletter.

Popsicles

Sources: Adapted from information from *Dinner's in the Freezer* by
Jill Bond and *Whole Foods for the Whole Family Cookbook*.

Pudding Pops

Make the recipe for homemade pudding on the next page, but use
1½ times the milk (a mixture of reconstituted dry and skim, or all
skim) required. Mix well. Pour into popsicle molds and freeze.

Gelatin Pops

Prepare your favorite gelatin recipe (see Recipe Index, or follow
directions on a store-bought box, regular or sugar-free). Use 1½
times the water called for in the recipe. Pour into popsicle molds and
freeze.

Yogurt Pops

Combine:

- **2   cups plain nonfat yogurt**
- **1   cup juice (apple, grape, orange, etc.)**
- **1   tablespoon honey**
- **1   teaspoon vanilla**

Beat with a whisk until smooth. Pour into popsicle molds and freeze.

Variations: The sky's the limit here! Try these suggestions: Puree
overly ripe bananas and add to popsicles. Use up leftover fruit juice,
nectar, bits of fruit, or "flopped" puddings or yogurt. Alternate a layer
of gelatin mixture with a different-colored layer, perhaps some all-
fruit spread. Shake milk in a jelly jar that's nearly empty, mixing the
last of the jelly with the milk. Etc., etc.!

Tips: If you you don't have popsicle molds and can't find any at
yard sales, pour above mixtures into little paper cups, freeze for an
hour, then insert wooden sticks into the partially set mixture. Or pour
the mixture into metal baking pans, making a thin layer, and freeze
(grown-ups will probably prefer a "slush" rather than a "pop!").

Nutritional Data: Too hard to figure with all the variations! Trust me, these are healthy *and* cheap.

Pudding

Serves 6

Source: A recipe from a cornstarch box and my own trial-and-error.

Place in a large, heavy-duty saucepan:

2   cups skim milk
2   cups water
1   cup dry milk powder
⅔ cup sugar
2   tablespoons sifted cocoa

Mix well with a wire whisk. Turn on medium heat and place pan on hot burner. Stir occasionally. Into a small container, pour and measure:

¾ cup water
6   tablespoons cornstarch (a little less than ½ cup)

Put on tight-fitting lid. Shake container until cornstarch and water are completely mixed, with no lumps. Stir cornstarch mixture into hot milk mixture. Stir constantly for several minutes, until pudding begins to thicken. Cook and stir for another two minutes. Remove from heat. Stir in:

1   teaspoon vanilla

Serve hot or cold.

Variations: For vanilla pudding, omit cocoa and add ⅛ cup sugar. For banana pudding, add three mashed bananas to the vanilla pudding recipe.
Tips: This pudding takes some time, but the taste is so much better than store-bought, it's worth it. Ask one of your older children or your spouse to do the stirring while you cook the rest of the meal.

Nutritional Data for One Serving Chocolate Pudding (1 Cup): Calories: 191, Calories from Fat: 4, Total Fat: 0g, Saturated Fat: 0g, Cholesterol: 4mg, Sodium: 109mg, Total Carbohydrate: 41g, Dietary Fiber: 0g, Sugars: 25g, Protein: 7g, Vitamin A: 13%, Vitamin C: 2%, Calcium: 25%, Iron: 4%

Smoothy-Frothy

Serves 4 to 6

Source: Adapted from a recipe in *Dinner's in the Freezer*
by Jill Bond.

Place in a blender:

1 to 2 cups frozen fruit: bananas, strawberries, blueberries, etc.

1 to 2 cups yogurt, milk and/or fruit juice

Fill the rest of the pitcher with ice. Blend until smooth.

Variations: Try different combinations of fruits, relying most on those in season (and cheapest).

Tips: Jill says, "Your liquid to fruit ratio will determine whether you're eating a 'milkshake' or 'ice cream'. . . . We keep bananas frozen in our freezer for these low calorie treats. Peel the bananas first and cut them in two-inch sections. Freeze in an airtight container."

Nutritional Data: Too hard to figure!

Strawberry "Pudding"

Serves 8

Source: Adapted from a recipe by Jan Kent, author of *A Taste of Dutch* cookbook.

Into a blender, pour:

½ cup water

Sprinkle over the top:

2 envelopes unflavored gelatin

Let stand 3 to 4 minutes. Bring to a boil:

1   cup skim milk

Pour into blender. Process at low speed until gelatin is completely dissolved, about two minutes. Add and process at high speed:

⅓   cup sugar
1   teaspoon almond (or vanilla) extract
½ to 1 quart strawberries, stemmed and halved

Pour into dessert dishes or a bowl. Chill until set.

Variations: One teaspoon sugar substitute can be used in place of sugar. Use an equal amount of seasonal fruit or mixed fruit instead of strawberries.

Tips: Be careful not to let the boiling milk overflow and make a mess!

Nutritional Data for One Serving (⅔ cup): Calories: 67, Calories from Fat: 2, Total Fat: 0g, Saturated Fat: 0g, Cholesterol: 1mg, Sodium: 19mg, Total Carbohydrate: 14g, Dietary Fiber: 1g, Sugars: 13g, Protein: 3g, Vitamin A: 2%, Vitamin C: 55%, Calcium: 5%, Iron: 2%

Swedish Apple Pudding with Custard Sauce

Serves 6

Source: *Healthy Exchanges Food Newsletter.**

18   (2½" X 2½") graham crackers
3   cups unsweetened applesauce
1½   teaspoons JO's Apple Pie Spice**
1   (4 serving) pkg Jell-O sugar-free vanilla cook and serve pudding mix
2   cups skim milk

*Note: The format of this recipe differs from most others in this book at JoAnna Lund's—the author's—request that her original recipe remain exactly as it appeared in her newsletter.
**See Resources, "Miscellaneous Products and Videos," on how to order JO's Spices.

1   **teaspoon vanilla extract**
1   **tablespoon reduced-calorie margarine**

Preheat oven to 350 degrees. Place 9 graham crackers in a 9X9 inch cake pan. Spoon 1½ cups applesauce over crackers. Sprinkle ½ teaspoon JO's Apple Pie Spice over applesauce. Place 6 crackers evenly over top. Spoon remaining applesauce over crackers and sprinkle with another ½ teaspoon JO's Apple Pie Spice. Crush remaining 3 crackers and sprinkle cracker crumbs evenly over top. Bake 45 minutes. About 10 minutes before apple pudding is done, combine dry pudding mix and skim milk in a medium saucepan. Cook over medium heat, stirring constantly with wire whisk, until mixture thickens and starts to boil. Remove from heat. Stir in vanilla extract, reduced-calorie margarine and remaining ½ teaspoon JO's Apple Pie Spice. Let apple pudding cool 2 to 3 minutes. For each serving, place apple pudding on dessert dish and top with ⅓ cup warm custard sauce.

Serves 6
Each serving equals:
HE: 1 Bread, 1 Fruit, ⅓ Skim Milk, 13 Optional Calories
186 Calories, 2 gm Fat, 4 gm Protein, 38 gm Carbohydrate, 281 mg Sodium, 2 gm Fiber
Diabetic: 1½ Starch, 1 Fruit

HINT: 1) Also good with apple pudding cold and sauce warmed in microwave.
2) Substitute any reputable brand for JO's Apple Pie Spice.
3) 2 tablespoons chopped walnuts can be sprinkled on top with remaining cracker crumbs.

Recipe Permissions

Applesauce Gingerbread recipe reprinted with permission from *Secrets of Fat-Free Baking* by Sandra Woodruff. Copyright 1994, $12.95. Published by Avery Publishing Group, Inc., Garden City Park, New York, 1-800-548-5757.

Bagels recipe reprinted with permission from *Cheap Eating* by Pat Edwards, Upper Access Books, Copyright 1993, Hinesburg, VT.

Baked Fruity Chicken recipe reprinted with permission from *The $30 a Week Grocery Budget, Volume I* by Donna McKenna (author and publisher, no copyright date), Casco, ME.

Banana-Cranberry Muffins recipe reprinted with permission from *Healthy Exchanges Food Newsletter* by JoAnna M. Lund (author and publisher), Copyright 1995, DeWitt, Iowa.

Beef and Noodle Soup recipe reprinted with permission from *Healthy Exchanges Food Newsletter* by JoAnna M. Lund (author and publisher), Copyright 1995, DeWitt, Iowa.

Breakfast Biscuits recipe reprinted with permission from *Healthy Exchanges Food Newsletter* by JoAnna M. Lund (author and publisher), Copyright 1995, DeWitt, Iowa.

Caramel Apricot Rice Pudding recipe reprinted with permission from *Healthy Exchanges Food Newsletter* by JoAnna M. Lund (author and publisher), Copyright 1995, DeWitt, Iowa.

Cheesy Tuna Garden Skillet recipe reprinted with permission from *Healthy Exchanges Food Newsletter* by JoAnna M. Lund (author and publisher), Copyright 1995, DeWitt, Iowa.

Cornbread (Muffins) recipe reprinted with permission from *A Taste of Dutch* cookbook by Jan Kent (author and publisher, no copyright date), Berger, MO.

Crystallized Grapes and Oranges recipe reprinted with permission from *Cheap Eating* by Pat Edwards, Upper Access Books, Copyright 1993, Hinesburg, VT.

Dragon Sauce recipe reprinted with permission from *Dinner's in the Freezer* by Jill Bond, Great Christian Books Publishing, Copyright 1995, Elkton, MD.

Easy Baked Beans recipe reprinted with permission from *Cheap Eating* by Pat Edwards, Upper Access Books, Copyright 1993, Hinesburg, VT.

Florida Cracker Lemonade recipe reprinted with permission from *Dinner's in the Freezer* by Jill Bond, Great Christian Books Publishing, Copyright 1995, Elkton, MD.

French Toast recipe reprinted with permission from *The $30 a Week Grocery Budget, Volume I* by Donna McKenna (author and publisher, no copyright date), Casco, ME.

Golden Broccoli Salad recipe reprinted with permission from *Healthy Exchanges Food Newsletter* by JoAnna M. Lund (author and publisher), Copyright 1995, DeWitt, Iowa.

Greek Feta Salad recipe reprinted with permission from *Healthy Exchanges Food Newsletter* by JoAnna M. Lund (author and publisher), Copyright 1995, DeWitt, Iowa. 1995, Dewitt, Iowa.

Hamburger Stroganoff recipe reprinted with permission from *The $30 a Week Grocery Budget, Volume I* by Donna McKenna (author and publisher, no copyright date), Casco, ME.

Maple Waldorf Fruit Salad recipe reprinted with permission from *Healthy Exchanges Food Newsletter* by JoAnna M. Lund (author and publisher), Copyright 1995, DeWitt, Iowa.

Micah's Cornbread (Cornbread Muffins in this book) recipe reprinted with permission from *A Taste of Dutch* Cookbook by Jan Kent (author and publisher, no copyright date), Berger, MO.

Minestrone recipe reprinted with permission from *Cheap Eating* by Pat Edwards, Upper Access Books, Copyright 1993, Hinesburg, VT.

Momwiches recipe reprinted with permission from *A Taste of Dutch* Cookbook by Jan Kent (author and publisher, no copyright date), Berger, MO.

O'Brion's Irish Dish recipe reprinted with permission from *The $30 a Week Grocery Budget, Volume II* by Donna McKenna (author and publisher, no copyright date), Casco, ME.

Orange Sherbert recipe reprinted with permission from the April 1994 issue of *The Penny Pincher* newsletter by Jackie Iglehart (author and publisher), Copyright 1994, Kings Park, NY.

Pineapple Torte recipe reprinted with permission from *Healthy Exchanges Food Newsletter* by JoAnna M. Lund (author and publisher), Copyright 1995, DeWitt, Iowa.

Popovers recipe reprinted with permission from *The $30 a Week Grocery Budget, Volume I* by Donna McKenna (author and publisher, no copyright date), Casco, ME.

Popsicles recipe reprinted with permission from *Dinner's in the Freezer* by Jill Bond, Great Christian Books Publishing, Copyright 1995, Elkton, MD.

Potato Chowder recipe reprinted with permission from *A Taste of Dutch* Cookbook by Jan Kent (author and publisher, no copyright date), Berger, MO.

Pretzels recipe reprinted with permission from *Cheap Eating* by Pat Edwards, Upper Access Books, Copyright 1993, Hinesburg, VT.

Saucy "Faux" Steaks recipe reprinted with permission from *Healthy Exchanges Food Newsletter* by JoAnna M. Lund (author and publisher), Copyright 1995, DeWitt, Iowa.

Scalloped Potatoes recipe reprinted with permission from *Cheap Eating* by Pat Edwards, Upper Access Books, Copyright 1993, Hinesburg, VT.

Smoothy-Frothy recipe reprinted with permission from *Dinner's in the Freezer* by Jill Bond, Great Christian Books Publishing, Copyright 1995, Elkton, MD.

Stuffing recipe reprinted with permission from *Cheap Eating* by Pat Edwards, Upper Access Books, Copyright 1993, Hinesburg, VT.

Susan Thomas's Casserole recipe reprinted with permission from *Dinner's in the Freezer* by Jill Bond, Great Christian Books Publishing, Copyright 1995, Elkton, MD.

Swedish Apple Pudding With Custard Sauce recipe reprinted with permission from *Healthy Exchanges Food Newsletter* by JoAnna M. Lund (author and publisher), Copyright 1995, DeWitt, Iowa.

Sweet 'N' Sour Meatballs recipe reprinted with permission from *Dinner's in the Freezer* by Jill Bond, Great Christian Books Publishing, Copyright 1995, Elkton, MD.

Turkey Burgers recipe reprinted with permission from *Cheap Eating* by Pat Edwards, Upper Access Books, Copyright 1993, Hinesburg, VT.

Very Best Fudge Brownies (Fudge Brownies in this book) recipe reprinted with permission from *Secrets of Fat-Free Baking* by Sandra Woodruff. Copyright 1994, $12.95. Published by Avery Publishing Group, Inc., Garden City Park, New York, 1-800-548-5757.

Wheat Thins recipe reprinted with permission from the October 1992 issue of *The Penny Pincher* newsletter by Jackie Iglehart (author and publisher), Copyright 1992, Kings Park, NY.

PEAK SEASON FOR FRUITS & VEGETABLES

	JAN	FEB	MAR	APR	MAY	JUN	JUL	AUG	SEP	OCT	NOV	DEC
FRUIT												
Apples									▓	▓	▓	▓
Apricot						▓	▓	▓				
Avocados			▓	▓	▓	▓	▓	▓				
Bananas			▓	▓		▓	▓					
Blackberries						▓	▓					
Blueberries						▓	▓					
Cherries						▓						
Cranberries										▓	▓	
Grapefruit	▓	▓										▓
Grapes								▓	▓	▓		
Lemons						▓	▓					
Melons								▓	▓			
Nectarines							▓	▓				
Oranges	▓	▓	▓					▓				▓
Peaches							▓	▓				
Pears								▓	▓	▓		
Pineapples				▓	▓							
Plums						▓	▓					
Raspberries						▓	▓					
Strawberries				▓	▓							
Tangerines	▓											▓
Watermelon						▓	▓					
VEGETABLES												
Artichokes			▓	▓								
Asparagus				▓	▓							
Green Beans							▓	▓				
Beets						▓	▓			▓		
Broccoli	▓	▓								▓	▓	▓
Brussel Sprouts	▓									▓	▓	▓
Cabbage					▓							
Carrots	▓	▓	▓	▓	▓	▓	▓	▓	▓	▓	▓	▓
Celery	▓	▓										
Corn							▓	▓		▓		
Cucumber					▓		▓	▓		▓		
Eggplant							▓	▓		▓		
Lettuce						▓						
Mushrooms									▓	▓	▓	
Onions					▓	▓						
Green Onions						▓	▓	▓				
Peas			▓	▓					▓	▓		
Peppers								▓	▓	▓		
Potatoes	▓	▓	▓	▓	▓	▓	▓	▓	▓	▓	▓	▓
Pumpkins										▓	▓	
Spinach			▓	▓								
Tomatoes							▓	▓				
Winter Squash									▓	▓	▓	▓

Reprinted with permission from *The Frugal Times*, September 1992

CHAPTER 7

Final Words

As of this writing, we have lived in our "new" rental house for four years. We're continuing to budget $50 to $53 a week for healthy food, and most of the time, staying within that budget. Some days it seems almost impossible to spend so little. That's when I remind myself of why we limited ourselves in the first place: in order to transfer dollars from grocery bills to higher-priority areas, such as housing.

I spent about $57 on food this week. I wasn't well-organized, and simply overshot my goal. Although we make mistakes, Michael and I continue to try and contain the dollar amount we've set for groceries. It seems the children are eating more every day! I've heard legendary stories about teenagers and the amount of food they consume. It isn't going to be easy, sticking to this budget.

On the other hand, I am excited about the information I've been able to share with you in *Eat Healthy For $50 a Week*. A combination of money-saving techniques and hard work is essential, if any of us are going to keep our grocery bills at half the national average. But I am convinced this task is not impossible.

Again, $50 a week may be an unrealistic figure for some of you. And perhaps not all of the strategies and cost-cutting ideas apply to your situation; they don't all apply to ours! What I have tried to show is that there are many different approaches to saving money on groceries. I am confident that you will be able to discover what works best for you, and adjust your lifestyle accordingly.

A final chapter should point out that these pages are certainly not the final *word*. I hope to hear from many of you who are more expert than I at saving money on food: write and tell me about any good ideas, healthy recipes, or techniques you know (and I don't). Perhaps one of these days, another book will follow from all the new information you've shared.

In the meantime, let me leave you with a checklist to encourage you as you tackle the important job of cutting back on your food budget. What could you do, starting today? What could you do next week? Next month? Nobody will be able to—or want to—do everything on the list. But like our hypothetical Price family, implementing one small step at a time will make a major difference in the amount of money you're spending on groceries. When you add up the savings, it is my sincere hope that you will be able to afford some of the goals in your life.

CHECKLIST FOR SAVINGS

- Set up a budget for groceries and plan to spend that total amount weekly.
- Visit several different stores over a period of a few weeks in order to compare prices.
- Assemble a notebook that lists each store's prices on products you buy regularly.
- Make a detailed, well-planned weekly list.
- Clip coupons and combine them with specials at a double-coupon store.
- Watch for good refund offers on foods you buy, then redeem them.
- Look over a refunding magazine to see if large-scale refunding and couponing appeals to you.
- Resolve to shop once a week or less when possible.
- Stick to your list when you shop.
- Eliminate impulse buying.
- Buy generic or store-brand products whenever possible.
- Buy in bulk. This may be as simple as stocking up on supermarket specials.
- Utilize THE PANTRY PRINCIPLE™.
- Buy produce that is currently in season.
- Stock up on fresh, seasonal fruits and vegetables at a pick-your-own place.

- Stock up on candy right after Halloween, Christmas, and other holidays.
- Never pay full price, wherever you shop.
- Call around to find alternative food sources in your area.
- Shop at a warehouse store.
- Shop at a dairy.
- Shop at a cheese outlet.
- Shop at a health food store for some items like spices.
- Shop at a day-old bread store.
- Shop at a produce stand.
- Shop at a meat market that offers special values on meat.
- Shop at a farmers' market.
- Try to buy everything on special when you shop at the supermarket.
- Eliminate most convenience foods from your meals.
- Start making some foods, such as salad dressings and croutons, from scratch.
- Bake your own bread, by hand or with a breadmaker.
- Prepare some recipes in large quantities so "convenience foods" are ready in the freezer.
- Make out monthly menu plans.
- Do most of your cooking once every two to four weeks.
- Mega-cook® several of the same kinds of meals in large quantities.
- Keep a careful watch of leftovers and use or freeze excess amounts weekly.
- Resolve to try 24-hour-in-advance meal planning for most efficient use of foods on hand.
- Do 15-minute cooking to save both time and money on healthy meals.
- Substitute a balanced variety of other foods for large helpings of meat.
- Serve smaller portions of expensive foods.
- Serve larger portions of healthy, filling foods like brown rice, beans, and whole grain breads.
- Replace nonnutritious foods, like sugary desserts and white bread, with nutritious ones, like low-fat custards and whole wheat bread.
- Substitute less expensive breakfast items, like oatmeal or toast with all-fruit spread, for donuts and fancy cereals.

- Drink water, brewed tea, and fruit juice rather than boxed fruit drinks, coffee, and soda.
- Eat less.
- Brown bag your family's lunches.
- Start a garden.
- Consider becoming a member of a garden club or association.
- If you lack garden space, look into alternatives, such as square-foot gardening, sharing an urban garden space or planting in containers.
- Visit your library or County Extension Service for free information on gardening, as well as a number of other topics.
- Learn how to preserve your own food through canning, freezing, and other techniques.
- Be on the lookout for gleaning possibilities.
- Barter for food with friends and neighbors.
- Call SHARE headquarters to learn if the organization has a branch in your area.
- Join a commercial bartering exchange (or at least call and find out more).
- Join a cooperative.
- Entertain economically.
- Eat more meals at home.
- Limit the amount of money spent on meals away from home.
- Find out if your family is eligible for any government programs.
- Read other books and newsletters that will help you to save on your grocery bills.
- Remember *why* you're trimming your grocery bill: to free up extra money, so that you can begin to realize some of the dreams in your life. Good luck!

APPENDIX 1
More Real-Life Shopping Lists and Menu Plans

One week's shopping list and some menu plans are described in Chapter One. For those of you who want to know more about how I shop and cook, here are three additional, consecutive weeks of actual lists and the menus that followed.

SHOPPING LIST #2

From Aldi

3 gallons ½% milk
2 dozen eggs
3 16-ounce loaves whole wheat bread
2 9-ounce bags pretzels
1 18-ounce jar peanut butter
1 pound dry pinto beans
2 pounds brown sugar
1 2-ounce bottle pure vanilla
1 14-ounce box marshmallows and stars cereal
1 18-ounce box cornflakes
19 bananas
1 pound part-skim mozarella cheese

2 8-ounce containers low-fat yogurt
1 small box corn muffin mix
1 16-ounce box soda crackers
1 6-ounce can water-packed tuna
5 pounds white flour
1 12-ounce can condensed milk
1 32-ounce bottle ketchup
1 15-ounce box toasted oats cereal
1 head lettuce
2 12-ounce cans frozen orange juice

Total: $30.73

From Shop 'n' Save

2 pounds yellow popcorn
1 8-ounce can baking powder
1 11-ounce container "lite" (low
    sodium) salt
1 16-ounce jar low-fat Miracle
    Whip
1 16-ounce can pumpkin
1 8-ounce container whipped
    topping
1 pound low-fat whipped
    margarine

5 pounds whole wheat flour
1 8-ounce container baking
    cocoa
1 10-ounce bottle soy sauce
1 16-ounce bottle fat-free salad
    dressing
1 head fresh spinach
1 8-ounce carton yogurt
½ gallon ice milk

Total: $16.81

From a nearby convenience store
1 pound M&M's

Total: $3.21

From Ben Franklin
60 penny candies

Total: $.62

Grand Total: $51.37

This week I shopped at Aldi as usual. Their private label mozzarella cheese, packaged in eight-ounce bags, is actually cheaper per ounce than a co-op's bulk buy cheese. (I can't say that it necessarily tastes better, but it does cost less.) The same is true of Aldi's pretzels in 12-ounce bags; they're cheaper than Sam's Club's version. This was one of the surprising discoveries I made when first comparing prices.

My second stop was at a discount supermarket. Shop 'n' Save's everyday prices are among the lowest in town, and I had an accumulated list of items that aren't stocked at Aldi. I chose mostly generic and private label foods, and also bought name brand, low-fat margarine, salad dressing, whipped topping, and ice milk on sale at 30 to 50 percent off.

Our refrigerator was still well stocked with all the fruits and vegetables given to us the week before, so there was no need to visit my favorite produce stand.

And now, a true confession: one night this week, we bought M&M's at a nearby Quik Trip, and we paid full price for them! Michael and I made cookies, and we all ate some, and they weren't one bit healthy! Which goes to prove my point: don't follow us as an example. We try, but we're not perfect!

WEEKLY MENUS #2

Tuesday

B: Whole wheat toast, scrambled eggs, milk
S: Bananas
L: Leftover chicken and stuffing*, yogurt*, 3 penny candies, milk
S: Popcorn and orange juice
D: Veggie pizza* with tomatoes, green peppers, onions, and mushrooms, lettuce and sprouts* salad, pumpkin pie* with nonfat whipped topping, Kool-Aid or tea

Wednesday

B: Cold cereal with milk
S: Apples
L: Leftover pizza*, applesauce, animal crackers, 3 penny candies, milk
S: Watermelon slices
D: Broiled salmon croquettes*, broiled eggplant*, coleslaw*, carrot coins, homemade whole wheat bread, reduced-fat oatmeal cookies*, water or tea

Thursday

B: Oatmeal or oatmeal bread, milk
S: Watermelon slices
L: Grilled cheese sandwiches (made with low-fat cheddar), pretzels, yogurt*, 3 penny candies, milk
S: Bananas
D: Stir-fry* chicken with cauliflower, broccoli and carrots, brown rice, coleslaw*, sliced tomatoes, bread sticks*, M&M cookies

Friday

B: Cinnamon toast, scrambled eggs, milk
S: Orange juice and popcorn
L: Peanut butter and jelly sandwiches, watermelon slices, graham crackers, 2 M&M cookies, milk
S: Apples or bananas
D: Enchiladas* with (some) ground turkey, tomatoes and zucchini,

lettuce and tomato cubes, mozzarella cheese, steamed peas, corn muffins*, M&M cookies, water or tea

Saturday

B: Oatmeal pancakes*, milk
S: Frozen fruit* slush
L: Leftover macaroni and cheese, leftover enchiladas*, pretzels, milk
S: Sliced bananas and grapes
D: Chicken and whole wheat noodles*, oatmeal bread, corn, cauliflower slices, low-fat ice cream, orange juice

Sunday

B: Cold cereal with milk
S: Pretzels
L: Chili* with low-fat cheese and saltines, leftovers (oatmeal bread, lettuce, cauliflower and slaw), milk
S: Sliced watermelon and bananas
D: Carry-out pizza, carrot sticks, caramel corn*, Kool-Aid or tea

Monday

B: Whole wheat banana muffins* (same recipe as the banana bread), milk
S: Apples
L: Leftover chili*, peanut butter crackers, banana muffins*, caramel corn*, milk
S: Watermelon slices
D: Tuna salad* with sprouts on whole wheat bread, hashbrown potatoes and zucchini*, steamed peas, low-fat chocolate pudding*, water or tea

Remember I told you that we try to use up all our leftovers? This week shows how. I served leftovers for several lunches, and recycled vegetables into the hashbrown/zucchini mixture, chicken stir-fry, pizza, enchiladas, and chili. Christian and Lisa pick out anything they can't identify in a dish (not always an easy task), but the rest of us enjoy the extra flavor of these "surprise veggies."

By now you may realize that I offer many of the same breakfasts, snacks, and lunches repeatedly. That's because, at dinner, we sometimes try new things, and my children *hate* to try new things. (Do yours?) We like to keep the rest of their meals as enjoyable as possible, with foods that they really like. Also, when we have a perishable food on hand, like watermelon, I serve it often so it doesn't spoil and go to waste.

In Chapter One, I mentioned my use of alternative strategies. One of them is cooking and baking double or triple batches of a recipe, and freezing the excess. The oatmeal cookies mentioned in these menus came from my freezer. I also decided to make my own whole wheat noodles for the chicken and noodles dish; they were just too expensive in the supermarket. My recipe made a huge batch, and I froze a big bowlful for chicken soup the following week.

Why the pizza, pumpkin pie, and Kool-Aid on Tuesday? That was Michael's birthday, and I prepared some of his favorites. (I *know* it's a strange combination.) Enough said. By the way, the pizza listed on Sunday was one medium Pizza Hut special we got for *$2*.

SHOPPING LIST #3

From Aldi

3 gallons ½% milk
2 dozen eggs
1 8-ounce bag tortilla chips
1 16-ounce box soda crackers
1 18-ounce jar peanut butter
2 pounds brown sugar
1 32-ounce bottle ketchup
1 17-ounce box bran flakes
  cereal
6 pounds apples
5 quarts sherbert
1 pound part-skim mozzarella
  cheese

Total: $31.92

2 9-ounce bags pretzels
1 pound graham crackers
1 15-ounce box raisins
2 packages taco shells (10 per
  package
5 pounds white flour
1 14-ounce box puffed cocoa
  cereal
1 whole frozen chicken
2 12-ounce cans frozen orange
  juice

From Frontier IGA

2   packages (10 each) chicken
    hot dogs
4+ pounds ground beef

Total: $5.96

From Wonder Hostess (day-old bread store)

1 16-ounce loaf rye bread   2 16-ounce loaves 100% whole
1 8-pack English muffins   wheat bread
1 8-pack hamburger buns   2 8-pack hot dog buns
1 10-pack low-fat Twinkies   1 16-ounce box animal crackers

Total: $2.97

From a local florist

4 pounds tomatoes

Total: $1.00

From Vaccaro & Sons Produce

1 whole pineapple   6 peaches
5 oranges   18 bananas
2 pounds grapes   2 pounds green beans
1 pound carrots   1 whole garlic

Total: $8.48

From Ben Franklin

60 penny candies

Total: $.62

Grand total: $50.95

This was a six-store week! That's very unusual for me, as I make it
a point not to go far out of my way or make several stops. But I did
have good reasons.

First, the day-old bread outlet was right on my way to IGA. When
this store offered a half-off coupon on everything in stock, I just
couldn't pass it up. Notice my total, and the amount of food I bought,
at Wonder. (By the way, at the time I recorded these menus, I usually
made a loaf of bread daily in my breadmaker, and supplemented with
store-bought bread. Now I'm making much more from scratch.)

We were all in the mood to barbeque, and IGA's ground beef and
chicken hot dogs are some of the best in town. Both were on sale,
too. En route home, I stopped by a floral shop whose front sign
advertised four pounds of tomatoes for $1 (I sent the boys in). Next,
to the produce stand, then Aldi. Shopping time was still around two
hours.

WEEKLY MENUS #3

Tuesday

B: Omelet, toast, milk
S: Watermelon slices
L: Graham crackers with peanut butter, apple slices, pretzels, 3 penny candies, milk
S: Fresh peaches
D: Grilled burgers* and chicken hot dogs, baked beans*, lettuce salad with sprouts*, veggie platter with sliced onions, tomatoes and lettuce leaves, low-fat Twinkies, Kool-Aid or tea

Wednesday

B: Cold cereal with milk
S: Bananas
L: Nachos with cheese and salsa, oranges, animal crackers, 3 penny candies, milk
S: Apples
D: Baked fruity chicken* with brown rice and onions, homemade whole wheat bread, steamed broccoli, sliced tomatoes, sherbet cones, water or tea

Thursday

B: Whole wheat banana bread*, oatmeal, milk
S: Grapes or apples
L: Leftover chicken hot dogs, pretzels, animal crackers, 3 penny candies, milk
S: Watermelon slices
D: Cabbage rolls*, mashed potatoes* and low-fat gravy*, popovers*, reduced-fat oatmeal cookies*, water or tea

Friday

B: English muffins, toast, scrambled eggs, milk
S: Apples
L: Cheese tortillas, graham crackers, 3 penny candies, milk
S: Ice cream cones (out)
D: Barbequed chicken* with sprouts* and tomatoes on whole

wheat bread, carrot coins, cauliflower slices, fresh pineapple, watermelon, water or tea

Saturday

B: Breakfast out (lots of fruit at a breakfast bar)
S: None
L: Peanut butter and jelly sandwiches, pretzels, bananas, milk
S: Watermelon slices
D: Hamburger pot pie* (with lots of cabbage and onion), home-made oatmeal bread, sliced tomatoes, lettuce salad with sprouts*, sherbert cones, milk (for the children), water or tea

Sunday

B: Cold cereal with milk
S: Graham crackers
L: Chicken noodle vegetable soup*, whole wheat poppy seed muffins*, carrot slices, licorice, milk
S: Orange juice
D: Oatmeal pancakes*, peanut butter apples, fresh pineapple, water

Monday

B: Oatmeal with milk
S: Apples
L: Leftovers from yesterday's lunch, milk
S: Popcorn and orange juice
D: Dinner out (including baked fish and salad bar)

I cooked with more red meat this week than usual, so let me explain how I prepared the dishes involved. First, the hamburgers were grilled, letting excess fat drip into the fire, and we adults had small servings. Cabbage rolls and hamburger pot pie both had very small amounts of meat; instead, I loaded them up with cabbage, onion and/or potatoes instead. From four pounds of ground beef purchased this week, these three recipes used a total of less than three pounds: two pounds for hamburgers, and a half pound each for the other two dishes. (And remember there are six of us!) In this way, fat content and cost are kept to a minimum while flavor is maximized.

Breakfast, lunch, and snacks listed in these menus are always what the children and I eat, and depending on Michael's schedule, *may* be what he eats (if not to his liking, my husband raids the fridge and pantry for his own meals). Dinner is nearly always shared together. On Sunday, we ate our main meal at lunch when we returned from church, and a lighter meal in the evening. Michael doesn't care for pancakes, so while the children and I feasted on those, he ate fruit and cold cereal instead.

You may recall that I often bake and cook ahead, and this week I took advantage of some of my surplus. Several foods came from the freezer: whole wheat banana bread, oatmeal cookies, and whole wheat noodles for chicken noodle vegetable soup. (See Chapter Three for once-a-month cooking and mega-cooking® techniques.)

The store-bought ice cream cones (Friday) were free: the children earned coupons from a summer reading program. Licorice (Sunday) was a gift from a neighbor.

We do eat out—once a week, ordinarily—but this week it happened to be twice (actually, my recording spanned half of two calendar weeks, and we went out once per calendar week). I don't count this as part of food spending for two reasons. First, we consider it family entertainment. Second, our total cost for a restaurant meal ranges from $4 (for breakfasts) to $10 (for dinners), tip included. We have arranged a barter with a local restaurant, an exchange of our services for nearly free meals once a week.

SHOPPING LIST #4

From Aldi

3 gallons ½% milk
2 8-ounce containers yogurt
2 16-ounce loaves whole wheat bread
1 13-ounce box animal crackers
5 pounds white flour
2 pounds brown sugar
1 15-ounce box fruit rings cereal
1 17-ounce box bran flakes
1 pound frozen peas

2 dozen eggs
1 pound margarine
1 8-ounce bag tortilla chips
1 16-ounce package fig bars
4 pounds white sugar
1 6-ounce can water-packed tuna
1 18-ounce box cornflakes
1 whole frozen chicken
1 pound frozen broccoli
12 bananas

1 pound fresh carrots
6 pounds apples
Total: $28.90

2 12-ounce cans frozen orange
juice

From National
1 pound fat-free margarine
2 6-ounce packages low-fat
sliced turkey
1¾ pounds grapes
Total: $8.53

1 10-ounce bag Bavarian
pretzels
9 pounds potatoes

From Vaccaro & Sons Produce
1 whole pineapple (free)
10 oranges
2 pounds green beans
Total: $8.09

14 bananas
1 whole cauliflower
1 red onion

From Ben Franklin
60 penny candies
Total: $.62

Grand total: $46.14

Ordinarily we don't buy lunch meat, but this week I was able to get a name brand, low-fat variety for half price. I also got odd-sized potatoes at 50 percent off, and a free pineapple when I explained that the one I bought last week was partly spoiled inside.

Some of you may wonder, with these lists of basic, "unprepared" foods, if I spend all my time in the kitchen. Actually, cooking is rather low on my priority list compared to home-schooling and working at my business. Leftovers and goods from the freezer are my "convenience foods." I also rely heavily on fast, easy recipes. That's why our breakfasts ordinarily require five to ten minutes preparation; lunches, the same; and dinner, 15 to 40 minutes. It's a rare day when I'm cooking in the kitchen for more than one hour total.

WEEKLY (OR PART OF A WEEK, AT LEAST!) MENUS #4

Tuesday

B: English muffins, toast, scrambled eggs, milk
S: Apples
L: Peanut butter graham crackers, pretzels, carrot sticks, 3 penny candies, milk
S: Sherbet cones
D: Baked ham, twice-baked potatoes*, Jell-O with fresh pineapple and bananas, sliced tomatoes, leftover lettuce, steamed peas, fig bars, water

Wednesday

B: Cold cereal with milk
S: Bananas
L: Sliced turkey (low-fat lunch meat) sandwiches, pretzels, licorice, milk
S: Fresh peaches
D: Cheesy tuna (tuna in homemade cheese sauce) on whole wheat toast, brown rice, broccoli, sliced tomatoes, carrot coins, apple crisp*, water or tea

Only two days of menus are recorded this week, because my 21 days are up, and also because we left to go out of town shortly afterward. So let me use these six meals to describe "two days in the kitchen with Rhonda;" it may help you to see how I prepare nutritious food quickly.

Tuesday: Breakfast is self-explanatory. How long does it take to scramble three eggs? I fixed toast and English muffins at the table while we ate. The children had apples for snacks (washed carefully, of course). Lunch and afternoon snack required about 10 minutes total preparation time.

Dinner was easy: I put the ham in a baking pan, ladled on a thawed sauce from the freezer (leftover from the last ham), and placed it in the oven. Potatoes were prepared the day before, Crock-Potted, mashed and filled. I made plain Jell-O in the morning while the children were busy with their math workbooks at our kitchen table. Everything else was sliced or diced or steamed just before we ate.

I should explain that I have help with dinner every night. Eric, Christian, and Lisa take turns being "Junior Chef." This not only makes cooking much easier, but also more enjoyable. Total food preparation time for the day: about 45 minutes.

Wednesday: Talk about simple meal plans! Breakfast, lunch, and two snacks totaled 15 minutes, tops. At dinner, Eric opened a can of tuna for me and I made a quick, low-fat cheese sauce. We took accumulated bread pieces out of the freezer, arranged them on an aluminum pan, and baked the "toast." Freezer rice was thawed in the microwave. Broccoli was steamed, carrots cut up. Apple crisp required the most time, a little more than 15 minutes because of slicing all that fruit. Total food preparation time for the day: about 55 minutes.

See, I told you this doesn't take long! And the food is healthy, and cheap, too!

APPENDIX 2

Membership Warehouses and Wholesale Clubs: More Information

If you're seriously considering joining a membership warehouse or wholesale club (the names are basically synonymous), you should know more about what they are, how they operate, and where they are located.

First, the *what*. Membership warehouses and wholesale clubs are businesses that make most of their profits through membership fees. Their retail prices are low because they normally mark up merchandise about 10 percent—compared to 25 percent or more for discount chains, and 50 percent and up for other retailers—above cost.

How? Wholesale clubs eliminate middlemen—plus all of the expenses of both distributors and additional freight—by shipping goods directly from the manufacturer to their warehouses. They also save by minimizing the number of salespeople and eliminating fancy fixtures. Costs are cut to the bone in order to keep prices low. To make up for lost profits, membership warehouses charge fees to "qualified" individuals who want to shop their stores. Qualifications are so broadly defined that almost anyone can participate.

Where do you find a wholesale club? If you live in a large metropolitan area, simply pick up your telephone white pages and check under one of the following companies' names. You can also contact the home office. If for example, you live in Mayville, Oregon, and have no PriceCostco in your town, call PriceCostco's headquarters to find out if there's a store within easy driving distance. Although the following list looks slim, remember these are huge companies, each with dozens of stores nationwide. One is probably already in your area or will be in the near future.

BJ's Wholesale Club, One Mercer Road, Natick, MA 01760. Tel. 1-800-BJS CLUB.

PriceCostco, Inc., 10809 120th Avenue NE, Kirkland, WA 98033. Tel. (206) 828-8100.

Sam's Wholesale Club, 702 Southwest Eight Street, Bentonville, AR 72716. Tel. 1-800-925-6278.

Warehouse Club, 7235 N. Linder Avenue, Skokie, IL 60077. Tel. (708) 679-6800.

APPENDIX 3

Kitchen Machines—Yes or No?

Because I own a breadmaker, I'm often asked whether or not I recommend them for everyone else. The question is, are they—and other sophisticated kitchen machines, for that matter—really worth the money? Do they pay for themselves? What are the advantages and disadvantages?

Amy Dacyczyn recently wrote an interesting article in *The Tightwad Gazette*. The title, "Read This Article and Save $150,000"[1] summed up Amy's main point: that we sometimes buy into the line that we're *saving*, but exactly *what* and *how* are we saving? Let me explain how I think this relates to buying expensive kitchen equipment.

In Chapter Three, you read about Jackie Iglehart bartering her graphic design skills for a seltzer-maker. At one time the Igleharts were purchasing about $200 worth of store-bought seltzer every year. Their machine retailed for $250, so the initial investment cost was absorbed in a little over a year. Now that the seltzer-maker is paid for, the family spends about eight cents per liter—or $47 a year—for seltzer. They save $153 compared to what they used to buy.[2]

But what if the Igleharts gave up seltzer altogether, and drank only ice water? In that case, they would "save" much more, in the long run, than they are now. They would not have had to barter time for a seltzer-maker, nor keep paying to have their CO_2 canister filled occasionally. They also wouldn't have to purchase another machine when this one eventually gives up the ghost.

What About Breadmaking Machines (Autobakeries)?

I doubt that I would have bought a breadmaker for myself, but ours was a very generous gift from friends. I have to admit I love the convenience of having a fresh-baked loaf of bread ready in less than three hours. My machine has a timer that enables me to program the loaf to finish up to 12 hours after I set it. It's wonderful to wake up to homemade bread for breakfast, or to have it waiting for dinner at the end of a hectic day.

On the other hand, I don't think the flavor or texture of machine bread is quite as good as hand-baked bread. I've found that my family tires of the sameness rather quickly, no matter how much I change the recipe. Ingredients used are limited, in that very little whole grain flours can be substituted for white in my particular model, Hitachi; in other words, the resulting bread is mostly white. Also, measurements must be *very* exact, and even then, bread can "flop" on humid days or for some reason.

Writers of thrift newsletters are divided on this subject. Jackie Iglehart thinks autobakeries are more than worth the investment. As I mentioned earlier in this book, Jackie buys bulk flour, spices, and yeast at a discount, and uses her breadmaker to make 15-cent loaves. She says her machine has paid for itself in a year, and now the Igleharts are saving a considerable amount of money.[3]

Amy Dacyczyn of *The Tightwad Gazette* disagrees. Rather than buying a new breadmaker, Amy suggests purchasing a secondhand bread bucket from a yard sale, or using a food processor (if you already own one), to make bread. She also recommends buying day-old loaves from discount bakeries. Amy doesn't believe a bread machine saves time (if you bake quick recipes in quantity) or money. One of her concerns stems from the high initial investment cost; she also wonders if an autobakery will last much longer than the time required to pay for itself. As you might guess, the Dacyczyns make most of their bread from scratch.[4]

Should you buy a bread machine? Ask yourselves these questions to help find the answer for you and your family:

Do I *need* a breadmaker?

Will I use it often enough to justify the investment?

Do I like the taste of the loaves? Do other family members also like the taste?

Can I afford it?

Is it worth it to me to spend the money on an autobakery rather than on something else?

If you answered "no" to some or all of these questions, you should seriously consider making your own bread or buying from a day-old bread store. If you answered all "yes", go out and buy yourself a machine! And enjoy it!

How Can I Make Cheap, *Healthy* Bread?

My breadmaker cost around $170 at Sam's Club, and if you're considering one, this is probably the kind you have in mind. There are other, more expensive machines that give you healthier loaves. You can, for example, purchase an autobakery that processes 100 percent whole grain flour, for $200 to $300. Another help is the use of a heavy-duty mixer ($400 to $500); this machine combines ingredients and kneads dough so quickly and thoroughly that little rising time is required. In other words, you throw in the ingredients, and the heavy-duty mixer does all the hard work. All you have to do is to wait for the kneading to finish, place the dough in pans and bake: fresh loaves (or cinnamon rolls, pizza crusts, etc.) in 75 to 90 minutes, start to finish.[5] Very convenient, but expensive!

For maximum nutrition, you might consider buying a grain mill. Mills convert whole grains into whole grain flour, which in turn makes all-whole grain bread. The biggest drawbacks to milling are the cost of the equipment (electric high-speed mills range from $250 to $300) and the noise (they're *loud*). Hand-operated models are available for $75 to $125, but grind very slowly.

Recently at a home-school fair, I got a chance to see an electric grain mill in action, and later taste the bread made with milled flour. *I* liked the flavor and texture, but no-one else in my family did. Looks like the Barfields will have to make healthy bread some other way, at least for now! By the way, I know of some families who use the hand-operated mills, and the mills are operated by the children as part of their weekly chores. The manually operated method does take a *long* time.

Whether you make use of whole grains and a mill or simply buy whole grain flour, I think the best way to get inexpensive, healthy bread is to make it from scratch, by hand. Consider this: my machine bread averages about 20 to 25 cents per loaf. But I can hand-bake *healthier* bread for about 28 cents. (And this does not include factoring in the investment cost of a machine.) What I've tried lately, with great success, is to whip together a huge batch of bread or muffins, serving one batch for dinner, then freezing the rest for future meals. I honestly can't tell much (if any) difference between fresh breads and those reheated in the oven or microwave. And if 90-Minute Cinnamon Yeast Bread recipe (see Recipes) takes 25 minutes mixing time for five loaves, my time invested per loaf is five minutes each, exactly what I spend assembling the ingredients in the bread machine.

What it really comes down to is this: is the convenience and/or healthy benefit of an autobakery, seltzer-maker, grain mill, or other high-tech machine worth the investment to you? Could you use alternative recipes and strategies instead? I won't presume to answer. This has to be an individual decision. I do caution you to investigate thoroughly before you make a major investment: find someone who owns a kitchen machine, watch it in action, and taste the resulting foods yourself before you purchase anything. Research the most recent annual buying guide of *Consumer Reports* (available in any library); they'll tell you which models give you the most for your money.

And by the way, if you're curious to know Amy Dacyczyn's answer to her article's teaser, "Read This Article and Save $150,000," the answer is: "Don't buy a Rolls-Royce."

NOTES

1. From *The Tightwad Gazette,* March 1995 (#58). See Resources.

2. For further reading, order back issue #6 (November/December 1992) of *The Penny Pincher.* See Resources.

3. For further reading, order back issue #5 (September/October 1992) of *The Penny Pincher.* See Resources.

4. For further reading, order back issue #39 (August 1993) of *The Tightwad Gazette.* See Resources.

5. Both Joyful Living Distributors and The Urban Homemaker offer autobakeries, heavy-duty mixers, grain mills, and many other kitchen machines as part of their large inventory of products. See Resources, Miscellaneous Products, and Videos.

RESOURCES

Books, Booklets, Brochures

All About Vegetables
Ortho's comprehensive publication (©1990, 160 pages, $8.95 paperback) is just what it is says it is, *All About Vegetables* and how to grow them. The book is available in retail stores nationwide, including K-Mart, Builders Square, and many others.

Baker's Easy Cut-Up Party Cakes
This full-color, 95-page booklet shows you how to make professional-looking homemade cakes, then cut, assemble, and decorate them. The results are so incredible, your child will never ask for a store-bought birthday cake again! (Use my low-fat cake recipe, and you'll *really* come out ahead.) Send $2.50 plus your name and address (zip required) to Kraft General Foods USA, P.O. Box 4114, Kankakee, IL 60902, or call 1-800-435-0917 for more information.

Ball Blue Book® Guide to Home Canning, Freezing and Dehydration
Pick up a copy of this $4.95 book at Wal-Mart or selected hardware and grocery stores, wherever Ball® products are sold. Or send $4.95 + $1.00 p&h to Alltrista Corporation, Direct Marketing Department, P.O. Box 2005, Muncie, IN 47307-0005. You'll learn nearly everything you need to know about preserving food.

The Best of Cheapskate Monthly, Simple Tips For Living Lean in the '90s

Mary Hunt, editor of *Cheapskate Monthly* newsletter, details a 200-page plan for turning your finances around. Features include a step-by-step program for getting out of debt and staying there, plus information on subjects as diverse as coupons, cheap home remedies and cleaners, managing mortgages, raising financially responsible kids, and more. The book is available in all bookstores and wherever paperback books are sold (St. Martin's Press, ©1993, $4.50).

Cheap Eating

Pat Edwards describes her book as a way to "feed your family well and spend less." *Cheap Eating* (©1993, 201 pages, $9.95) goes into more detail than *Eat Healthy* on growing and preserving your own food, plus other money-saving tips and strategies. There are also several excellent low-cost recipes. Call Upper Access Books, 1-800-356-9315, for ordering information.

The Cheapskate Monthly Money Makeover

Mary Hunt's second book (©1995, St. Martin's Press, $4.50) emphasizes the need for a money makeover that works. Mary shares her own techniques, sound financial principles, and advice from hundreds of readers who went from being in the red to having more money, assets, and financial security. Available in bookstores.

DC Super Heroes Super Healthy Cookbook

Mark Saltzman, Judy Garlan, and Michele Grodner have compiled a 100-page classic cookbook of "good food kids can make themselves." Full-color photographs, easy instructions, and superhero cartoons on nearly every page inspire young cooks to head for the kitchen. This book is no longer in print, but your local library may either have a copy on hand or locate one through interlibrary loan. (While you're looking, browse through other children's cookbooks.)

Dinner's in the Freezer!

With 256 pages in an 8½ X 11 inch format, *Dinner's in the Freezer!* (©1993) is a comprehensive home management system with detailed information on prepreparing food. Jill Bond, author, shares her expertise as a mega-cook® who often prepares up to six months' worth of economical, nutritious meals. The book costs $17 (plus s&h) through Great Christian Books. Call 1-800-775-5422 to order.

Enchanted Broccoli Forest: And Other Timeless Delicacies
Mollie Katzen wrote a 320-page vegetarian cookbook in 1982 that "veggie" friends of mine cite as one of their all-time favorites. Ten Speed Press in Berkeley, California, still publishes this book for $16.95 (paperback). Available in bookstores.

Extending the Table . . . A World Community Cookbook
Written in the same format as *More-with-Less Cookbook,* Joetta Handrich Schlabach presents recipes from countries around the world, most of them low-cost, nutritional, and very interesting. Order her collection (332 pages, Herald Press, ©1991, $15.95) through your local Christian bookstore, or call 1-800-759-4447 (add $2.50 s&h if ordering by mail).

15-Minute Cooking
Rhonda Barfield's book describes her own system of cooking in just two 15-minute sessions daily, one in the morning and one just before dinner. You'll read about four weeks of typical, easy menu plans, as well as all the details you'll need to create your own. There are also dozens of new recipes (ones that aren't included in this book). Learn how to alternate these recipes (and your own), save money, cut your preparation time to the minimum, and still serve really tasty, home-cooked meals every day. $12.95, 200 pages, ©1995. To order, write to Rhonda at her company, Lilac Publishing, P.O. Box 665, Dept. EH, St. Charles, MO 63302-0665.

Food—Your Miracle Medicine: How Food Can Prevent and Cure Over One Hundred Symptoms and Problems
I've checked out this book from the library so many times, I've nearly worn it out. Jean Carper, author and medical researcher, cites hundreds of scientific studies on foods that are particularly healthy (see title!). Fascinating reading, this book really helped motivate us to eat better. Published by HarperCollins, ©1993, 576 pages, $13 (paperback), available in bookstores.

Gardening By Mail: A Sourcebook
Barbara J. Barton's detailed sourcebook lists all kinds of gardening supplies available through mail order. You'll find this Houghton Mifflin book (©1986, 288 pages, $16.45 paperback) in most bookstores.

Healthy Exchanges Cookbooks
JoAnna M. Lund, author, describes her collections as "common folk" healthy cookbooks. If you tried the sugar-free, low-fat, low-sodium recipes I borrowed from JoAnna (with permission), I'm sure you know what she means. Call 319-659-8234 for customer service, or 1-800-766-8961 for credit card orders and current prices. JoAnna will tell you about her books as well as her newsletter of the same name.

How To Save Money On Just About Everything
William Roberts's 200+ page book is out of print as of this writing, but may be available through libraries (request interlibrary loan, if necessary). By the time *Eat Healthy* is published, *HTSMOJAE* may also be carried in bookstores. The information in Appendix Two of this book is derived from Chapter 21, "Warehouse Membership Club," of Bill's book.

More-with-Less Cookbook
Doris Janzen Longacre's cookbook is subtitled "suggestions by Mennonites on how to eat better and consume less of the world's limited food resources." Over 300 pages of recipes and information, the book costs $15.95 (Herald Press, 41st printing, 1993). This popular classic can be found in most Christian bookstores, or call 1-800-759-4447 (add $2.50 s&h if ordering by mail).

The New LEAN Toward Health
This informative, free booklet is available from Project LEAN (Low-Fat Eating For America Now, sponsored by The American Dietetic Association's National Center for Nutrition and Dietetics). Subtitled "Quick, Easy, and Delicious Ways To Reduce the Fat in Your Diet," *The New LEAN Toward Health* "gives some practical tips to help make low-fat eating an everyday habit . . . things to do when shopping for food, cooking, and eating out." See American Dietetic Association for ordering information.

Once-a-Month Cooking
Written by Mimi Wilson and Mary Beth Lagerborg, *Once-a-Month Cooking* (©1992, 160 pages) describes "A Time-Saving, Budget-Stretching Plan To Prepare Delicious Meals." Detailed menus and shopping lists tell all you need to know for shopping and meal preparation, two to four weeks at a time. Send a donation of $10 (postage and handling included) to Focus on the Family Publishing, Colorado Springs, CO 80995, or call 1-800-232-6459.

The Ortho Problem Solver
This huge, encyclopedic resource volume contains a listing of every County Extension Service (CES) in the U.S. You'll also want to refer to it for answers to over 2,000 gardening problems, especially those related to pests and diseases. Photos illustrate each section. You can find *Ortho Problem Solver* at many home and garden centers and some hardware stores.

Party Panic (The Hesitant Homemaker's Guide To Planning The Perfect Dinner)
This self-published, 24-page booklet features a "checklist for planning dinner parties, table setting diagrams, seasonal themes, arrangements, placecards, invitations, 'mood makers' " and more. Melinda Tyler's advice *inspires* me to entertain, and her ideas include some wonderfully economical suggestions. To order, send $4.50 + $1.50 p&h to Melinda Tyler, P.O. Box 90, Dept. EH, Cottleville, MO 63338.

Putting Food By
Janet Greene has assembled a comprehensive book (512 pages, ©1988) that tells you all you need to know about preserving your food. Published by Viking Penguin, it's available in or through major bookstores for $9.95 (paperback).

Saving Money Any Way You Can
Here's a fast-paced book that covers nearly every imaginable money-saving topic. You'll find Mike Yorkey's informative volume (©1994, 319 pages) in Christian bookstores, or order through his publisher, Servant Publications, Box 8617, Ann Arbor, MI 48107, 1-800-458-8505.

Secrets of Fat-Free Baking

I reprinted two recipes from this delightful book in my Recipes section (with permission, of course). Sandra Woodruff's creations taste delicious, even without the fat. Published by Avery Publishing Group, Inc. (Garden City Park, NY, 1-800-548-5757), 232 pages, $12.95, ©1994. Check local bookstores or call Avery's toll-free number.

Square Foot Gardening

Mel Bartholomew's 347 page book shows you how to make the most of your garden space. This system seems both do-able and sensible, and the author gets you excited about trying. Highly recommended by gardeners I know. Published by Rodale Press (©1981, $16.95), it's available through local libraries, home and garden centers and bookstores.

A Taste of Dutch

This small cookbook contains several tasty recipes, some of which I've adapted for my Recipes section. Jan Kent charges only $3.50 + $1 s&h for her self-published gem. Send your order to Jan at Rt. 1 Box 112, Dept. EH, Berger, MO 63014.

Thrifty Business: 111 Money Saving Tips

Rhonda Barfield's *classic* booklet, 32 pages, tells you how to save on groceries, supplies, clothes, some major household purchases, and recreation. $5.00 includes postage and handling, plus a guarantee that you'll save at least $50 or your money back. Send a check or money order to TB, P.O. Box 665, Dept. EH, St. Charles, MO 63302-0665.

The $30 a Week Grocery Budget, Volume I
The $30 a Week Grocery Budget, Volume II

Donna McKenna's first volume (60 pages) sells for $5.00, the second, slightly-shorter volume for $4.50, postage and handling included, or $9.00 for both booklets. The first contains detailed information on how Donna feeds a family of six for $30 a week, the second, more general advice on saving money. Both books are worth the price if only for the low-cost recipes. Write to Donna at 106 Bedford Street, Dept EH, Statesboro, GA 30458.

The Tightwad Gazette: Promoting Thrift as a Viable Alternative Lifestyle
The first two years of this popular newsletter by Amy Dacyczyn are also in book form, ©1993, $9.95, Villard Books, available in bookstores.

The Tightwad Gazette II
This volume contains the next two years (©1995) of the newsletter by the same name, same author, same publisher, $9.99.

The Use-It-Up Cookbook
Lois Carlson Willand has written 190 pages, a "Guide for Minimizing Food Waste," (©1990) that show how to creatively recycle every food imaginable. Send $12.95 (tax and postage included) to Practical Cookbooks, 145 Malcolm Avenue S.E., Minneapolis, MN 55414.

Whole Foods for the Whole Family Cookbook
Edited by Roberta Bishop Johnson for La Leche League International, this is one of the best, most practical cookbooks featuring whole foods on the market (©1993, 302 pages). To order, call 708-519-7730, or write to La Leche League, 1400 North Meacham Road, P.O. Box 4079, Schaumburg, IL 60168-4079. Cost is $16.95 + $4.00 s&h.

Catalogs and Special Reports

Consumer Information Catalog
The U.S. government makes numerous publications available, free or at little cost, through this catalog. You'll find much information on food and nutrition. Write for the latest issue: Consumer Information Catalog, Pueblo, CO 81009.

Penny Pincher's Landscape Makeover
Jackie Iglehart's special report includes ten ways to save money on landscaping and gardening, *easy* composting instructions, how to plant an edible landscape, an interview with a landscape architect, listings of plants that do well in combination planting, and intensive planting. For $3, you receive both the report and a free sample of the newsletter. Write to The Penny Pincher, P.O. Box 809, Dept. EH, Kings Park, NY 11754.

Penny Pincher's Garden Harvest

This second report by Jackie Iglehart features easy time-saving short-cuts and money-saving ways to preserve the harvest, plus instructions and recipes for harvesting and preserving fruits, vegetables, herbs and edible flowers. Again, $3 includes both the report and a free sample of the newsletter. Write to the address on page 209.

Food Stores

Aldi Inc.

As of this writing, there are approximately 450 stores in 18 states. Call the divisional headquarters nearest you to find the closest store (please keep in mind that there may be additional stores and headquarters that have been added since this book was written):

Illinois, Batavia: 708-879-8100 (this is also the national headquarters, and can be called regardless of where you live)

Indiana, Greenwood: 317-885-0808
Indiana, Valparaiso: 219-464-2500
Iowa, Burlington: 319-753-6213
Kansas, Olathe: 913-764-8822
Missouri, O'Fallon: 314-278-4700
Ohio, Hinckley: 216-273-7351
Ohio, Springfield: 513-323-5500
Pennsylvania, Center Valley: 610-798-9200

Save-A-Lot Food Stores

This food chain is similar to Aldi, but carries a larger selection of foods than Aldi does *and* is located in some areas where Aldi is not. Currently there are 450 stores in 26 states, most of them east of the Mississippi, but also in Oklahoma and Texas. For more information, call the national headquarters at 1-800-346-3808.

Note: Aldi and Save-A-Lot are primarily located in midwestern, eastern and southern American states. To the best of my knowledge, similar stores do not exist in the western U.S. See the end of the Resources section for a listing of cooperative warehouses available nationwide.

Miscellaneous Products and Videos

Beating the High Cost of Eating Video
Barbara Salsbury, originator of THE PANTRY PRINCIPLE™, explains how to save a fortune at the grocery store and at home in this excellent 95-minute video (awarded four stars by ABC CLEO Video Rating Guide for Libraries). To order both the video and a 76-page worksheet packet (a $10 value, free) mail $29.95 + $5 s&h to Salsbury Enterprises, 1453 Maryann Drive, Santa Clara, CA 95050. California residents, add appropriate sales tax. For credit card orders, call 1-800-999-4494.

JO's Spices
JoAnna Lund (of Healthy Exchanges fame) has created a collection of seasoning blends containing no salt, sugar, wheat, or MSG. For information, write JO's Spices, c/o Oh Nuts, Inc., Rock Valley Plaza, 4020 Blackhawk Road, Rock Island, IL 61201, or call 309-786-8871 for more information.

Joyful Living Distributors
Bill and Kristy Bell's home business specializes in breadmakers, whole grain mills, kitchen systems, special foods, books, and much more. They'll send you complete information on what they carry if you enclose an SASE with your inquiry. Write to the Bells at 1601 Kelly Road, Aledo, TX 76008. Allow four weeks for a reply (the Bells have seven children and they home-school!).

The Urban Homemaker
Marilyn Moll rightly deserves her title as The Urban Homemaker. Write for her free catalog of bread-baking equipment, products for better health, and practical-skills books, and you'll see why. Send two stamps to Box 440967, Aurora, CO 80044 or call 1-800-55-BREAD.

Newsletters

Cheapskate Monthly
Mary Hunt writes an excellent newsletter that focuses on getting out—and staying out—of debt, based on Mary's personal experience. For a free newsletter sample, send $1 for postage and handling to *Cheapskate Monthly*, P.O. Box 2135, Dept. EH, Paramount, CA

90723-8135. To subscribe, send $15.95 (cash, check or money order only) for 12 issues or $29.95 for 24 issues.

Consumer Newsline®

This once-a-year free newsletter features detailed information on how to preserve (usually through canning) a particular food. To be placed on the mailing list, send your name, address, and request to Alltrista Corporation, Direct Marketing Department, P.O. Box 2005, Muncie, IN 47307-0005. (This is Ball's parent company.)

Healthy Exchanges Newsletter

JoAnna Lund, author of the *Healthy Exchanges Cookbooks,* also writes a monthly newsletter filled with no-sugar, low-fat, low-sodium recipes, and good advice. Send $26.50 for 12 issues plus a storage binder to *Healthy Exchanges,* P.O. Box 124, Dept. EH, DeWitt, IA 52742-0124. Credit card orders, call 1-800-766-8961.

Living Cheap News

Larry Roth's newsletter contains general information on ways to save money. I especially enjoy Larry's witty commentary. Send $1.00 and a self-addressed, stamped envelope for a sample copy, or $12 for a one year (10 issues) subscription, to Living Cheap Press, 7232 Belleview, Dept. EH, Kansas City, MO 64114.

The Penny Pincher™

Jackie Iglehart's informative newsletter helps people learn money-saving strategies that can save them thousands of dollars each year; she'll even give you an "estimated savings" for each article and idea. Send a long SASE and $1 for a newsletter sample. An annual subscription of 12 issues costs $15.00. Back issues cost $2 each: issue #6 includes an article on seltzer-makers, and #5 on bread machines. (For information on *ordering* a seltzer-maker, see "National Safety Association" in the *Organizations and More* section of this Resources chapter.) Write to *The Penny Pincher,* 2 Hilltop Rd., Mendham, NJ 07945-1215, or call 1-800-41 PENNY for Visa and Mastercard orders.

The Pocket Change Investor (formerly The Banker's Secret Bulletin)

A quarterly newsletter dedicated to helping readers save money on their debts, like credit card bills and mortgages, a two-year subscription costs $19.95. Or send $1 for a bulletin sample to Good Advice Press, Box 78, Dept. EH, Elizaville, NY 12523.

Refund Express
If you're interested in large-scale couponing and refunding, send $3 for a sample issue of *Refund Express* to Sandy Ennis, P.O. Box 179, Commerce, GA 30529.

Refunding Makes Cents! (RMC)
While you're at it, write to *RMC* for a slightly different approach to couponing and refunding. Send $2.95 for a sample issue to *RMC*, Michele Easter, Box R, Farmington, UT 84025.

Skinflint News
Ron and Melodie Moore pack all sorts of money-saving advice into their newsletter. Enclose an extra stamped, self-addressed envelope in your envelope, and receive a free newsletter sample. Or send $12 for an annual (12 issue) subscription to *Skinflint News*, Box 818, Dept. EH, Palm Harbor, FL 34682.

The Tightwad Gazette (newsletter)
Amy Dacyczyn, the self-proclaimed "frugal zealot," proves her claim true in her informative newsletter. Send a long SASE for a free sample, or $12 for 12 issues, to *The Tightwad Gazette*, RR1 Box 3570, Dept. EH, Leeds, ME 04263-9710. Back issues cost $1.00.

Organizations and More

American Community Gardening Association
To learn more about opportunities for shared urban gardening, write to ACGA at 325 Walnut Street, Philadelphia, PA 19106.

The American Dietetic Association's National Center for Nutrition and Dietetics
The Consumer Nutrition Hot Line, 1-800-366-1655, is a service where consumers may call, Monday through Friday, 8 A.M. to 8 P.M. (CST) to listen to recorded messages on current nutrition topics in Spanish and English. From 9 to 4 (CST), you can also speak in person with a registered dietitian or be referred to a registered dietitian in your area. When you call, you may ask about ordering a free copy of *The New LEAN Toward Health*.

Extension Service
Usually referred to as Cooperative Extension Service (CES), this division of the U.S. Department of Agriculture provides all sorts of free

and low-cost services to local citizens. You might have a sample of your garden soil—or your canner's pressure gauge—tested through a nearby CES. Or request one of their numerous, helpful publications. To contact a Cooperative Extension Service in your area, first check the phone directory under "Extension Service." If that doesn't help, try a subheading under "County Agencies." Or contact your local state university (CES is associated with each state's land-grant college or university; in Illinois, it's U. of I., for example, and the University of Missouri in my home state). If all else fails, go to a local home and garden center and take a look at Ortho Problem Solver, a huge resource book listing every CES in the U.S.

La Leche League
For information on breastfeeding, answers to breast-feeding questions, a free catalog and/or the location of a nearby chapter, call 1-800-LALECHE or 708-519-7730.

Library System
If you cannot find a book (or other material) at the local library, request an interlibrary loan. Staff members will first try to locate a copy of your request in libraries nearby, then within your county or state. Depending on the circumstances, they may even make a nationwide search if necessary. Usually there is only a small fee involved, and sometimes the search is free.

Another option is to ask your library to buy a particular book (video, CD, etc.). Libraries are often very open to customer requests, and will do their best to accommodate you. To ensure an even better chance that your request is honored, ask one or two friends to call and ask for the same item!

National Cancer Institute
To receive free brochures on nutrition, including the "5 a Day for Better Health" plan, call 1-800-4-CANCER.

National Commercial Exchange
To learn more about commercial bartering exchanges, including the National Association of Trade Exchanges, write to Richard Harris at National Commercial Exchange, 106 Four Seasons Center, Suite 107B, Chesterfield, MO 63017.

National Cooperative Business Association
For a free information packet on cooperatives and up-to-date information on cooperatives in your area, write to NCBA at 1401 New York Avenue, N.W., Suite 1100, Washington, DC 20005-2160.

National Council of State Garden Clubs
Write to the national headquarters at 4401 Magnolia Avenue, St. Louis, Missouri 63110-3492, or call 314-776-7574 for information on the club nearest you in your state.

National Safety Association
NSA sells water and air treatment systems, and is mentioned in this book because of their seltzer-maker. If you cannot locate a local distributor, call Kathy Martin in New York at 516-757-5088 for more information.

SHARE (Self Help & Resource Exchange)
This is the organization that offers discounted packages of groceries to qualified groups whose individuals work public service hours. Headquartered in San Diego, California, SHARE is currently located in 29 regions, some of them serving a several-states area: Arizona, California, Colorado, Connecticut, Florida, Georgia, Illinois, Indiana, Iowa, Kansas, Kentucky, Maryland, Massachusetts, Michigan, Minnesota, Nebraska, New Jersey, New Mexico, New York, North Carolina, Ohio, Pennsylvania, Rhode Island, South Carolina, Tennessee, Virginia, Washington, DC, West Virginia, Wisconsin and all of New England. New SHARE chapters are starting often, so call (619-525-2200) or write (6950 Friars Street, San Diego, CA 92108) to locate the SHARE nearest you.

U.S. Department of Agriculture (USDA): Center for Nutrition Policy and Promotion
For free information on a variety of nutritional subjects, write to USDA, Center for Nutrition Policy and Promotion, 14th and Independence Avenue, SW, Suite 240-E, Washington, DC 20250.

U.S. Cooperative Food Warehouses
The National Cooperative Business Association currently lists the following contacts as regional sources for co-op buying. If you find an address or phone number is no longer correct, please contact the NCBA for up-to-date information.

National

Frontier Cooperative Herbs
Box 299
Norway, IA 52318
319-227-7991
Serves the nation with
herbs and spice

Northeastern States

Northeast Cooperatives, Inc.
P.O. Box 8188, Quinn Road
Brattleboro, VT 05304
802-257-5856 or
1-800-334-9939
Serves CT, MA, NH, NY, RI,
VT

Hudson Valley Federation
6 Noxon Road
Poughkeepsie, NY 12603
914-473-5400
Serves, NJ, NY, PA

Southeastern States

Orange Blossom Warehouse
1601 N.W. 55th Place
Gainesville, FL 32606
904-372-7061
Serves FL, NC, SC

Midwestern States

Blooming Prairie
Warehouse, Inc. (two
locations)
2340 Heinz Road
Iowa City, IA 52240
319-337-6448

Blooming Prairie Natural
Foods
510 Kasota Avenue, SE
Minneapolis, MN 55414
612-378-9774
Serves IA, IL, KS, MI, MN,
MO, NE, ND, SD, WI

Federation of Ohio River
Cooperatives
320-E Outerbelt, Suite E
Columbus, OH 43213
614-861-2446
Serves IN, KY, MD, MI, NC,
OH, PA, VA, WV

North Farm Co-op
Warehouse (two locations)
204 Regas Road
Madison, WI 53714
608-241-2667 or
1-800-236-5880

North Farm Co-op
Warehouse
1505 N. Eighth Street
Superior, WI 54880
715-392-9862 or
1-800-236-9862
Serves IL, IN, MI, MN, MO,
OH, WI

Ozark Co-op Warehouse
Box 1528
Fayetteville, AR 72702
501-521-4920
Serves AR, AZ, GA, KS, LA,
MO, MS, OK, TN, TX

Western States

Associated Cooperatives,
Inc.
12250 San Pablo Avenue,
#155
Richmond, CA 94805-2453
415-232-1111
Serves other warehouses

NutraSource
4005 Sixth Avenue South
Seattle, WA 98108
1-800-33N-UTRA or
1-800-762-0211 (WA)
Serves AK, ID, OR, WA

Tucson Cooperative
Warehouse
350 S. Toole
Tucson, AZ 85701
602-884-9951
Serves AZ, CA, CO, NM,
NV, TX, UT

Food Guide Pyramid
A Guide to Daily Food Choices

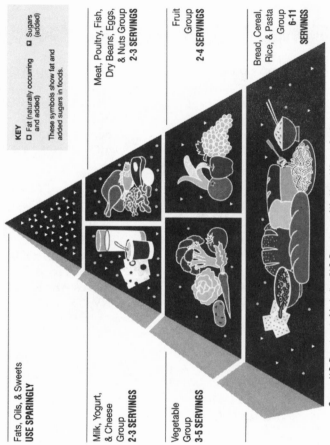

KEY
☐ Fat (naturally occurring and added)
☐ Sugars (added)

These symbols show fat and added sugars in foods.

Fats, Oils, & Sweets
USE SPARINGLY

Milk, Yogurt, & Cheese Group
2-3 SERVINGS

Meat, Poultry, Fish, Dry Beans, Eggs, & Nuts Group
2-3 SERVINGS

Vegetable Group
3-5 SERVINGS

Fruit Group
2-4 SERVINGS

Bread, Cereal, Rice, & Pasta Group
6-11 SERVINGS

Source: U.S. Department of Agriculture/U.S. Department of Health and Human Services

Other publications by Rhonda Barfield

15-Minute Cooking: $12.95 inc. p&h

200 page book. Strategies for preparing quick, easy, nutritious meals in only two 15-minute cooking sessions a day. Recipes, meal plans, much more.

Thrifty Business: 111 Money Saving Tips: $4 inc. p&h

32-page booklet. Introduction to saving money on food, clothing, major appliances, recreation, and more. *Save $50 on your household budget or your money back!*

Please send your check or money order with name, address, & phone # (just in case) to **Lilac Pub., P.O. Box 665, St. Charles, MO, 63302-0665.**

Name

Address

City   State   Zip

Phone

Items Ordered	Subtotal	
	Postage	
	MO residents add 7.22%	
allow 4-6 weeks delivery	Grand Total	

RECIPE INDEX